Study Guide

to accompany

Sociology:
A Brief Introduction

Eighth Edition

Richard T. Schaefer
DePaul University

Prepared by
Martha J. Warburton
University of Texas, Brownsville and Texas Southmost College

Rebecca Matthews
University of Iowa

and

Richard T. Schaefer
DePaul University

Boston   Burr Ridge, IL   Dubuque, IA   Madison, WI   New York   San Francisco   St. Louis
Bangkok   Bogotá   Caracas   Kuala Lumpur   Lisbon   London   Madrid   Mexico City
Milan   Montreal   New Delhi   Santiago   Seoul   Singapore   Sydney   Taipei   Toronto

The McGraw·Hill Companies

McGraw-Hill Higher Education

Study Guide to accompany
Sociology: A Brief Introduction
Richard T. Schaefer

1 2 3 4 5 6 7 8 9 0 QPD/QPD 0 9 8

ISBN 978-0-07-724002-8
MHID   0-07-724002-2

www.mhhe.com

CONTENTS

Introduction v

Chapter 1 1
Chapter 2 17
Chapter 3 36
Chapter 4 54
Chapter 5 71
Chapter 6 91
Chapter 7 107
Chapter 8 125
Chapter 9 143
Chapter 10 159
Chapter 11 177
Chapter 12 195
Chapter 13 212
Chapter 14 229
Chapter 15 247
Chapter 16 263

# INTRODUCTION

This study guide is designed to enhance your understanding of the discipline of sociology and to help you prepare for examinations covering *Sociology: A Brief Introduction*, 8th Edition, by Richard T. Schaefer. Careful use of this supplement will assist you in reviewing discussions of sociological theory, important research findings, and social policy sections.

The study guide has been developed specifically to provide you with a clearer understanding of the assigned material. The organization is identical to that of the textbook: Each chapter in the study guide corresponds directly to one of the 16 chapters in *Sociology: A Brief Introduction*, 8th Edition. Within each chapter of the study guide, the material is presented in the same sequence as in the textbook. Consequently, if you have problems with a particular subject or study guide exercise, you can return to the relevant pages in the text for further study.

You may find some sections of the study guide more helpful than others, but you should probably use all sections for the first few chapters until you learn what works best for you. Regardless of which sections you use, the study guide will be most valuable if you have read the textbook first. The purpose of the study guide is to assist you in reviewing the material after you have read an entire chapter of the text. We recommend waiting for a day *after* reading a chapter before turning to the study guide.

A *chapter outline* begins each chapter of the study guide. It presents the major topics of the chapter in the same order in which they appear in the text. If you review this outline and immediately recognize certain areas in which your comprehension is weak, you should probably return to the text before continuing your work with the study guide.

After the chapter outline there is a section of *key points*. In this section, short excerpts from the chapter are summarized in paragraph form with highlighted glossary items. These key points summarize the most important themes and concepts discussed in the chapter. They should be studied carefully before you proceed to later exercises in the study guide.

A list of *key terms* is included in each chapter of the study guide. Each glossary item is presented in the order in which it appears in the textbook. Space is provided so that you can test yourself by filling in the definition of each term. Although these key terms appear in boldface in the text, this section of the study guide offers another opportunity to reinforce your understanding of the basic concepts used by sociologists. You may be tempted to check them off as you think to yourself, "I remember that," but it is important to write out the answers in the study guide. The very act of writing them out will reinforce your mastery of these terms. Once you have finished, you can check your answers against the correct definitions, which are included in the same study guide chapter.

The *self-test* for each chapter allows you to examine your understanding of the text material. Each self-test includes 15 *modified true/false questions*, 25 *multiple-choice questions*, and 15 *fill-in questions*. Correct answers are provided for all sections of the self-test. Students will often ask, "Are the practice questions similar to the 'real' test questions?" The publisher materials for this course have been created in an integrated team approach. Therefore, if your instructor is using test material that is part of this package, there should be a high level of consistency between your Study Guide questions and the questions that you see on your tests.

To gain the greatest benefits from the self-test sections, do not use them after a hurried initial skimming of the chapter. Instead, use the self-test as a practice examination only after you have thoroughly studied the textbook material. As you take the test, note your weak areas; keep track of the questions on which you find yourself guessing. Recognize how you may be misreading or misinterpreting certain types of questions. After you check your answers, return to and reread the textbook passages where your comprehension was weak. Even if your instructor uses broad short-answer questions or essay questions on examinations, you will find the exercises in the self-test helpful in improving your understanding of the material in the textbook.

For each of the chapters in the textbook that ends with a social policy section, there is a corresponding exercise on *understanding social policy* in the study guide. These exercises ask questions about the social policy material in the text. Space is provided for your responses, and correct answers are included later in the study guide chapter.

In addition to this study guide, the *Reel Society Interactive Movie CD-ROM* included with your textbook and the Online Learning Center (the text's companion website) are valuable tools to help you study and master the material in the textbook. The CD-ROM features an interactive movie that demonstrates the sociological imagination through the use of actors and scenarios involving campus life. The program allows you to interact with the concepts described in the textbook in a relevant and meaningful context. A wide variety of issues and perspectives are addressed in order to relate major sociological concepts and theories to your everyday life. The Online Learning Center, located at www.mhhe.com/schaefer8, offers interactive quizzes and maps, social policy exercises, Census updates, chapter glossaries, vocabulary flashcards, and additional resources.

Effective use of the *Reel Society Interactive Movie CD-ROM*, the Online Learning Center Website, and this study guide, along with effective study habits, will ensure that your introduction to the discipline of sociology will be both meaningful and enjoyable.

1 UNDERSTANDING SOCIOLOGY

What Is Sociology?
   The Sociological Imagination
   Sociology and the Social Sciences
   Sociology and Common Sense

What Is Sociological Theory?

The Development of Sociology
   Early Thinkers
   Émile Durkheim
   Max Weber
   Karl Marx
   Modern Developments

Major Theoretical Perspectives
   Functionalist Perspective
   Conflict Perspective
   Interactionist Perspective
   The Sociological Approach

Applied and Clinical Sociology

Developing a Sociological Imagination
   Theory in Practice
   Research in Action
   Thinking Globally
   The Significance of Social Inequality
   Speaking across Race, Gender, and
      Religious Boundaries
   Social Policy throughout the World

Appendix: Careers in Sociology

BOXES
PHOTO ESSAY: *Are You What you Own?*
RESEARCH IN ACTION: *Looking at Sports from Three Theoretical Perspectives*
SOCIOLOGY IN THE GLOBAL COMMUNITY: *The Global Response to the 2004 Tsunami*

KEY POINTS

Sociology as a Field of Study: **Sociology** is the scientific study of social behavior and human groups. It focuses on social relationships, how those relationships influence people's behavior, and how societies develop and change.

The Sociological Imagination: In attempting to understand social behavior, sociologists rely on an unusual type of creative thinking. C. Wright Mills described such thinking as the **sociological imagination:** an awareness of the relationship between an individual and the wider society. A key element in the sociological imagination is the ability to view one's own society as an outsider would, rather than only from the limited perspective of personal experiences and cultural biases.

Sociology as a Science: The term **science** refers to the body of knowledge obtained by methods based upon systematic observation. Just like other scientific disciplines, sociology engages in organized, systematic study of phenomena (in this case, human behavior) in order to enhance understanding. In contrast to other social sciences, sociology emphasizes the influence that society has on people's attitudes and behavior and examines the ways in which people interact and shape society.

Sociological Theory: Within sociology, a **theory** is a set of statements that seeks to explain problems, actions, or behavior. An effective theory may have both explanatory and predictive power—that is, it can help us to see the relationships among seemingly isolated phenomena and to understand how one type of change in an environment leads to other changes.

Early Thinkers—Comte, Martineau, and Spencer: Auguste Comte (1798–1857) coined the term sociology to apply to the science of human behavior. He believed that a theoretical science of society and systematic investigation of behavior were needed to improve society. Harriet Martineau (1820–1876) offered insightful observations of the customs and social practices of both her native Britain and the United States. Herbert Spencer (1820–1903) adapted Charles Darwin's evolutionary view of the "survival of the fittest" by arguing that it is "natural" that some people are rich while others are poor.

Émile Durkheim: Émile Durkheim (1858–1917) was appointed as one of the first professors of sociology in France. Above all, Durkheim will be remembered for his insistence that behavior must be understood within a larger social context, not just in individualistic terms. Durkheim concluded that, like other forms of group behavior, religion reinforces a group's solidarity. Another of Durkheim's main interests was the consequences of work in modern societies.

Max Weber: Max Weber (1864–1920), a German sociologist, taught his students that they should employ *verstehen*, the German word for "understanding" or "insight," in their intellectual work. To fully comprehend behavior, we must learn the subjective meanings people attach to their actions; how they themselves view and explain their own behavior. We also owe credit to Weber for a key conceptual tool: the ideal type. In his own works, Weber identified various characteristics of bureaucracy as ideal types.

Karl Marx: In the analysis of Karl Marx (1818–1883), society was fundamentally divided between classes who clash in pursuit of their own class interests. When Marx examined the industrial societies of his time, he saw the factory as the center of conflict between the exploiters (the owners of the means of production) and the exploited (the workers). In *The Communist Manifesto*, which first appeared in 1848, Marx and Friedrich Engels (1820–1895) argued that the masses of people (whom they referred to as the *proletariat*) with no resources other than their labor should unite to fight for the overthrow of capitalist societies.

Charles Horton Cooley: Charles Horton Cooley (1864–1929) preferred to use the sociological perspective to look at smaller units of people—intimate, face-to-face groups, such as families, gangs, and friendship networks. He saw these groups as the seedbeds of society, in the sense that they shape people's ideals, beliefs, values, and social nature. Cooley's work increased our understanding of groups of relatively small size.

Functionalist Perspective: In the view of functionalists, society is like a living organism in which each part of the organism contributes to its survival. Therefore, the **functionalist perspective** emphasizes the way that parts of a society are structured to maintain its stability. For over four decades, Harvard University sociologist Talcott Parsons (1902–1979) dominated sociology in the United States with his advocacy of functionalism. Parsons saw any society as a vast network of connected parts, each of which contributes to the maintenance of the system as a whole.

Conflict Perspective: Where functionalists see stability and consensus, conflict sociologists see a social world in continual struggle. The **conflict perspective** assumes that social behavior is best understood in terms of conflict or tension between competing groups. Expanding on Marx's work, conflict theorists are interested in how society's institutions—including the family, government, religion, education, and the media—may help to maintain the privileges of some groups and keep others in a subservient position.

An African American View—W.E.B. Du Bois: One important contribution of conflict theory is that it has encouraged sociologists to view society through the eyes of those segments of the population that rarely influence decision making. Early Black sociologists, such as W.E.B. Du Bois (1868–1963), conducted research that they hoped would assist the struggle for a racially egalitarian society.

The Feminist View: The **feminist view** sees inequity in gender as central to all behavior and organization. Because it clearly focuses on one aspect of inequality, the feminist view is often allied with the conflict perspective. Those who hold to the feminist perspective tend to focus on the macro-level relationships of everyday life, just as conflict theorists do. Drawing on the work of Marx and Engels, contemporary feminist theorists often view women's subordination as inherent in all male-dominated societies.

Interactionist Perspective: The **interactionist perspective** generalizes about everyday forms of social interaction in order to understand society as a whole. It is a sociological framework for viewing human beings as living in a world of meaningful objects. These "objects" may include material things, actions, other people, relationships, and even symbols. George Herbert Mead (1863–1931) is widely regarded as the founder of the interactionist perspective.

Applied and Clinical Sociology: **Applied sociology** is the use of the discipline with the specific intent of yielding practical applications for human behavior and organizations. Often, the goal of such work is to assist in resolving a social problem. The growing popularity of applied sociology has led to the rise of the specialty of **clinical sociology**, which is dedicated to facilitating change by altering social relationships or restructuring social institutions. Applied and clinical sociology can be contrasted with **basic** (or pure) **sociology**, which seeks a more profound knowledge of the fundamental aspects of social phenomena.

Thinking Globally: Sociologists recognize that social behavior must be viewed in a global context. Today, developments outside a country are as likely to influence people's lives as changes at home. Some observers see globalization and its effects as the natural result of advances in communications technology, particularly the Internet and satellite transmission of the mass media. Others view it more critically, as a process that allows multinational corporations to expand unchecked.

KEY TERMS

Briefly define or identify the following terms in the spaces provided below. The definitions of these terms can be found later in this chapter of the study guide.

Sociology	Science
Sociological imagination	Natural science

Social science	Conflict perspective
Theory	Feminist view
Anomie	Interactionist perspective
Verstehen	Nonverbal communication
Ideal type	Dramaturgical approach
Macrosociology	Applied sociology
Microsociology	Clinical sociology
Functionalist perspective	Basic sociology
Manifest function	Globalization
Latent function	Social Inequality
Dysfunction	

SELF-TEST

MODIFIED TRUE/FALSE QUESTIONS: If the statement below is true, write "true" in the space provided. If the statement is false, briefly correct the error.

1.   Sociology is concerned only with how major social institutions like the government, religion, and the economy affect us.

2.   In the aftermath of natural disasters, a community's social organization and structure collapse.

3.   Émile Durkheim concluded that the suicide rates of a society reflected the extent to which people were or were not integrated into the group life of the society.

4.   French theorist Émile Durkheim coined the term *sociology*.

5.   The sociologist Harriet Martineau applied Charles Darwin's evolutionary concepts to societies.

6.   When Max Weber discussed the ideal bureaucracy, he was focusing on the best type of organization that was possible.

7.   Karl Marx argued that the working class needed to overthrow the existing class system.

8.   Émile Durkheim was a modern-day sociologist who focused on small groups.

9.   George Herbert Mead emphasized that sociology should strive to bring together the "macro-level" and "micro-level" approaches to the study of society.

10.   Microsociology concentrates on large-scale phenomena or entire civilizations.

11.   Talcott Parsons dominated sociology in the United States for over four decades with his advocacy of the interactionist perspective.

12.   Ida Wells-Barnett used her analysis of society as a means of resisting oppression. In her case, she researched what it meant to be African American, a woman in the United States, and an African American woman in the United States.

13.   Interactionists see symbols as an especially important part of human communication.

14.   George Herbert Mead is widely regarded as the founder of the interactionist perspective.

15.   Research by Greg Scott on the connection between illegal drug use and HIV/AIDS is an example of basic sociology.

MULTIPLE-CHOICE QUESTIONS: Read each question carefully and then select the best answer.

1. Sociology is
   a. an awareness of the relationship between an individual and the wider society.
   b. the scientific study of social behavior and human groups.
   c. concerned with what one individual does or does not do.
   d. very narrow in scope.

2. Sociology is concerned with
   a. social behavior and human groups.
   b. the behavior of an individual.
   c. random human actions.
   d. all of the above

3. Which of the following is most closely associated with the concept of the sociological imagination?
   a. Émile Durkheim
   b. Max Weber
   c. Karl Marx
   d. C. Wright Mills

4. Within sociology, a(n) _____ is a set of statements that seeks to explain problems, actions, or behavior.
   a. theory
   b. hypothesis
   c. operational definition
   d. correlation

5. In his study of suicide, Émile Durkheim was primarily concerned with
   a. suicide rates and how they varied from country to country.
   b. the personalities of individual suicide victims.
   c. the means people used to take their own lives.
   d. the effects of suicide on the families of victims.

6. In which sociologist's hierarchy of sciences was sociology the "queen" and its practitioners the "scientist-priests"?
    a. Auguste Comte
    b. Émile Durkheim
    c. Herbert Spencer
    d. Harriet Martineau

7. In *Society in America*, which early sociologist gave special attention to social class distinctions and to such factors as gender and race?
    a. Émile Durkheim
    b. Max Weber
    c. Auguste Comte
    d. Harriet Martineau

8. According to the text, Herbert Spencer
    a. applied the concept of evolution of the species to society.
    b. felt compelled to correct and improve society.
    c. argued that it is "unnatural" that some people are rich while others are poor.
    d. all of the above

9. Which sociologist introduced the concept of anomie to the discipline?
    a. Max Weber
    b. Herbert Spencer
    c. Émile Durkheim
    d. C. Wright Mills

10. Anomie refers to
    a. a construct, a made-up model that serves as a measuring rod against which actual cases can be evaluated.
    b. the study of small groups.
    c. the loss of direction felt in a society when social control of individual behavior has become ineffective.
    d. a set of statements that seeks to explain problems, actions, or behavior.

11. Which of the following concepts did Max Weber introduce to the field of sociology?
    a. dramaturgy
    b. the ideal type
    c. functionalism
    d. macrosociology

12. *The Communist Manifesto* was written by
    a. Karl Marx and Georg Hegel.
    b. George Herbert Mead and Jane Addams.
    c. Friedrich Engels and Karl Marx.
    d. Talcott Parsons and Robert Merton.

13. Which sociologist cofounded the famous Chicago settlement house called Hull House?
    a. Charles Horton Cooley
    b. Jane Addams
    c. George Herbert Mead
    d. C. Wright Mills

14. Robert Merton's contributions to sociology include
    a. successfully combining theory and research.
    b. an analysis of deviant behavior that focuses on societal goals and means.
    c. an attempt to bring "macro-level" and "micro-level" analyses together.
    d. all of the above

15. Which sociological perspective views society as a network of connected parts, each of which contributes to the maintenance of the system as a whole?
    a. the functionalist perspective
    b. the conflict perspective
    c. the interactionist perspective
    d. the dramaturgical perspective

16. _____ functions of institutions are open, stated, and conscious.
    a. Manifest
    b. Latent
    c. Dys
    d. Structural

17. A university that serves as a meeting ground for people seeking marital partners is performing
      a. a manifest function.
      b. a latent function.
      c. a dysfunction.
      d. a manifest dysfunction.

18. Karl Marx's view of the struggle between social classes inspired the contemporary
      a. functionalist perspective.
      b. conflict perspective.
      c. interactionist perspective.
      d. dramaturgical approach.

19. Which of the following was an early Black sociologist, active in the struggle for a racially egalitarian society, who was critical of theorists who seemed content with the status quo?
      a. Harriet Martineau
      b. Herbert Spencer
      c. Booker T. Washington
      d. W.E.B. Du Bois

20. The _____ perspective generalizes about everyday forms of social interaction in order to understand society as a whole.
      a. conflict
      b. functionalist
      c. interactionist
      d. feminist

21. In the 1990s, the workings of juries became a subject of public scrutiny. A sociologist would be most likely to use which perspective to gain a better understanding of the small-group setting of a jury deliberation room?
      a. interactionist
      b. conflict
      c. functionalist
      d. macrosociology

22. Erving Goffman's dramaturgical approach, which postulates that people present certain aspects of their personalities while obscuring other qualities, is derivative of what major theoretical perspective?
      a. the interactionist perspective

    b. the functionalist perspective

    c. the conflict perspective

    d. the feminist perspective

23. Sports perpetuate the false idea that success can be achieved simply through hard work, while failure should be blamed on the individual alone (rather than on injustices in the larger social system). This statement would most accurately represent which perspective?

    a. the functionalist perspective

    b. the conflict perspective

    c. the interactionist perspective

    d. the feminist perspective

24. Which sociological perspective examines sports on the micro level by focusing on how day-to-day social behavior is shaped by the distinctive norms, values, and demands of the world of sports?

    a. the functionalist perspective

    b. the conflict perspective

    c. the interactionist perspective

    d. the psychological perspective

25. Perhaps the major theme of analysis in sociology today is _____ : a condition in which members of society have differing amounts of wealth, prestige, or power.

    a. macrosociology

    b. the dramaturgical approach

    c. *Verstehen*

    d. social inequality

FILL-IN QUESTIONS: Fill in the blank spaces in the sentences below with the correct words. Where two or more words are required, there will be a corresponding number of blank spaces.

1. Sociology focuses primarily on the influence of _____ relationships on people's behavior and on how societies develop and change.

2. While the findings of sociologists may at times seem like common sense, they have been _____ by researchers.

3. _____ _____ noted that while suicide is a solitary act, it is related to group life, and that Protestants, unmarried individuals, and soldiers were more likely to commit suicide than Catholics, married individuals, and civilians.

4. In *Society in America*, originally published in 1837, English scholar _____ _____ examined religion, politics, child rearing, and immigration in the young nation.

5. _____ _____ adapted Charles Darwin's evolutionary view of the "survival of the fittest" by arguing that it is "natural" that some people are rich while others are poor.

6. _____ _____ concern for a value-free, objective sociology was a direct response to Marx's deeply held convictions.

7. _____ _____ pioneering work has led contemporary sociologists to focus on how membership in a particular gender classification, age group, racial group, or economic class affects a person's attitudes and behavior.

8. In the early 1900s, sociologist _____ _____ _____ saw smaller groups as the seedbeds of society.

9. Examinations of international crime rates, Émile Durkheim's cross-cultural study of suicide, and studies of population patterns of Islamic countries are all examples of _____. By contrast, research in which small groups are studied in laboratories is an example of _____.

10. _____ _____ saw society as a vast network of connected parts, each of which helps to maintain the system as a whole.

11. The university's role in certifying academic competence and excellence is an example of a _____ function.

12. In contrast to functionalists' emphasis on stability and consensus, _____ theorists view the social world as being in continuous struggle.

13. The _____ _____ draws on the work of Marx and Engels in that it often views women's subordination as inherent in capitalist societies.

14. _____ scholars have argued for a gender-balanced study of society which goes beyond the male point of view.

15. The _____ perspective would note that participation in sports might promote friendship networks that permeate everyday life.

DEFINITIONS OF KEY TERMS

Sociology: The scientific study of social behavior and human groups.

Sociological imagination: An awareness of the relationship between an individual and the wider society, both today and in the past.

Science: The body of knowledge obtained by methods based on systematic observation.

Natural science: The study of the physical features of nature and the ways in which they interact and change.

Social science: The study of the social features of humans and the ways in which they interact and change.

Theory: In sociology, a set of statements that seeks to explain problems, actions, or behavior.

Anomie: The loss of direction felt in a society when social control of individual behavior has become ineffective.

Verstehen: The German word for "understanding" or "insight"; used to stress the need for sociologists to take into account the subjective meanings people attach to their actions.

Ideal type: A construct or model for evaluating specific cases.

Macrosociology: Sociological investigation that concentrates on large-scale phenomena or entire civilizations.

Microsociology: Sociological investigation that stresses the study of small groups, often through experimental means.

Functionalist perspective: A sociological approach that emphasizes the way in which the parts of a society are structured to maintain its stability.

Manifest function: An open, stated, and conscious function.

Latent function: An unconscious or unintended function that may reflect hidden purposes.

Dysfunction: An element or a process of a society that may disrupt the social system or reduce its stability.

Conflict perspective: A sociological approach that assumes that social behavior is best understood in terms of conflict or tension between competing groups.

Feminist view: A sociological approach that views inequity in gender as central to all behavior and organization.

Interactionist perspective: A sociological approach that generalizes about everyday forms of social interaction in order to explain society as a whole.

Nonverbal communication: The sending of messages through the use of gestures, facial expressions, and postures.

Dramaturgical approach: A view of social interaction in which people are seen as theatrical performers.

Globalization: The worldwide integration of government policies, cultures, social movements, and financial markets through trade and the exchange of ideas.

Social inequality: A condition in which members of society have differing amounts of wealth, prestige, or power.

Applied sociology: The use of the discipline of sociology with the specific intent of yielding practical applications for human behavior and organizations.

Clinical sociology: The use of the discipline of sociology with the specific intent of altering social relationships or restructuring social institutions.

Basic sociology: Sociological inquiry conducted with the objective of gaining a more profound knowledge of the fundamental aspects of social phenomena. Also known as *pure sociology*.

ANSWERS TO SELF-TEST

Modified True/False Questions

1. Sociology is a very broad field of study. Sociologists are concerned with how major social institutions affect us, but they also study how other people influence our behavior, and how we ourselves affect other individuals, groups, and organizations.

2. In the aftermath of natural disasters, greater social organization and structure emerge to deal with a community's problems.

3. True

4. The term *sociology* was coined by Auguste Comte.

5. Herbert Spencer applied Charles Darwin's evolutionary concepts to societies.

6. When Max Weber discussed the ideal bureaucracy, he was providing a useful standard for measuring how bureaucratic an actual organization was.

7. True

8. Charles Horton Cooley was a modern-day sociologist who focused on small groups.

9. Robert Merton emphasized that sociology should strive to bring together the "macro-level" and "micro-level" approaches to the study of society.

10. Macrosociology concentrates on large-scale phenomena or entire civilizations. Microsociology stresses the study of small groups.

11. Talcott Parsons dominated sociology in the United States for over four decades with his advocacy of the functionalist perspective.

12. True

13. True

14. True

15. Research by Greg Scott on the connection between illegal drug use and HIV/AIDS, is an example of applied sociology.

Multiple-Choice Questions

1. b	10. c	19. d
2. a	11. b	20. c
3. d	12. c	21. a
4. a	13. b	22. a
5. a	14. d	23. b
6. a	15. a	24. c
7. d	16. a	25. d
8. a	17. b	
9. c	18. b	

Fill-In Questions

1. social
2. tested
3. Émile Durkheim
4. Harriet Martineau
5. Herbert Spencer
6. Max Weber's
7. Karl Marx's
8. Charles (Horton) Cooley
9. macrosociology; microsociology
10. Talcott Parsons
11. manifest
12. conflict
13. feminist view
14. Feminist
15. interactionist

CHAPTER 2

SOCIOLOGICAL RESEARCH

What Is the Scientific Method?
   Defining the Problem
   Reviewing the Literature
   Formulating the Hypothesis
   Collecting and Analyzing Data
   Developing the Conclusion
   In Summary: The Scientific Method

Major Research Designs
   Surveys
   Observation
   Experiments
   Use of Existing Sources

Ethics of Research
   Confidentiality
   Research Funding
   Value Neutrality

Feminist Methodolgy

Technology and Sociological Research

Social Policy and Sociological Research: Studying Human Sexuality
   The Issue
   The Setting
   Sociological Insights
   Policy Initiatives

Appendix I: Using Statistics, Tables, and Graphs
Appendix II: Writing a Research Report

BOXES
   RESEARCH TODAY: *Adolescent Sexual Networks*
   RESEARCH TODAY*: Polling in Baghdad*
   RESEARCH IN ACTION*: What's in a Name?*
   TAKING SOCIOLOGY TO WORK*: Dave Eberbach, Research Coordinator, United Way of Central Iowa*

| KEY POINTS

The Scientific Method: The **scientific method** is a systematic, organized series of steps that ensures maximum objectivity and consistency in researching a problem. There are five basic steps in the scientific method: defining the problem, reviewing the literature, formulating the hypothesis, selecting the research design and then collecting and analyzing data, and developing the conclusion.

Defining the Problem: The first step in any research project is to state as clearly as possible what you hope to investigate. An **operational definition** is an explanation of an abstract concept that is specific enough to allow a researcher to assess the concept.

Formulating the Hypothesis: After reviewing earlier research and drawing on the contributions of sociological theorists, the researchers formulate the **hypothesis**: a speculative statement about the relationship between two or more factors known as variables. A **variable** is a measurable trait or characteristic that is subject to change under different conditions. The variable hypothesized to cause or influence another is called the **independent variable**. The second variable is termed the **dependent variable** because its action "depends" on the influence of the independent variable.

Collecting and Analyzing Data: In most studies, social scientists must carefully select what is known as a **sample**. A sample is a selection from a larger population that is statistically representative of that population. The most frequently used sample is a **random sample** in which every member of the entire population being studied has the same chance of being selected.

Validity and Reliability: The scientific method requires that research results be both valid and reliable. **Validity** refers to the degree to which a measure or scale truly reflects the phenomenon under study. **Reliability** refers to the extent to which a measure provides consistent results.

Surveys: A **survey** is a study, generally in the form of an interview or questionnaire, which provides sociologists with information about how people think and act. Among the best-known surveys of opinion in the United States are the Gallup poll and the Harris poll. Surveys can be indispensable sources of information, but only if the sampling is done properly and the questions are worded accurately and without bias.

Observation: Investigators who collect information through direct participation and/or by closely watching a group or community are engaged in **observation**. This method allows sociologists to examine certain behaviors and communities that could not be investigated through other research techniques. In some cases, the sociologist actually joins a group for a period of time to gain an accurate sense of how it operates. This is called *participant observation*.

Experiments: When sociologists want to study a possible cause-and-effect relationship, they may conduct experiments. An **experiment** is an artificially created situation that allows the researcher to manipulate variables. In the classic method of conducting an experiment, two groups of people are selected and matched for similar characteristics, such as age or education. The **experimental group** is exposed to an independent variable; the **control group** is not.

Use of Existing Sources: Sociologists do not necessarily need to collect new data in order to conduct research and test hypotheses. The term **secondary analysis** refers to a variety of research techniques that make use of previously collected and publicly accessible information and data. Many social scientists find it useful to study cultural, economic, and political documents, including newspapers, periodicals, radio and television, tapes, the Internet, scripts, diaries, songs, folklore, and legal papers. In examining these sources, researchers employ a technique known as **content analysis**, which is the systematic coding and objective recording of data, guided by some rationale.

Ethics of Research: The American Sociological Association (ASA), the professional society of the discipline, first published the Code of Ethics in 1971. It includes the following basic principles: maintain objectivity and integrity in research, respect the subject's right to privacy and dignity, protect subjects from personal harm, preserve confidentiality, seek informed consent from research participants, acknowledge research collaboration and assistance, and disclose all sources of financial support.

Research Funding: Sometimes disclosing all the sources of funding for a study is not a sufficient guarantee of ethical conduct. Accepting funds from a private organization or even a government agency that stands to benefit from a study's results can call into question a researcher's objectivity and integrity.

Value Neutrality: Max Weber believed that sociologists must practice **value neutrality** in their research. In his view, researchers cannot allow their personal feelings to influence the interpretation of data. Investigators have an obligation to accept research findings, even when the data run contrary to their own personal views, to theoretically based explanations, or to widely accepted beliefs. The issue of value neutrality does not mean that sociologists can't have opinions, but it does mean that they must work to overcome any biases, however unintentional, that they may bring to their research.

Technology and Sociological Research: The increased speed and capacity of computers are enabling sociologists to handle larger and larger sets of data. Anyone with a desktop computer and a modem can access information and learn more about social behavior. The Internet is an inexpensive way to reach large numbers of potential respondents, and get a quick response. However, there are some obvious dilemmas: How do you protect a respondent's anonymity? How do you define the potential audience?

Studying Human Sexuality: The controversy surrounding research on human sexual behavior raises the issue of value neutrality, which becomes especially delicate when one considers the relationship of sociology to the government. The federal government has become the major source of funding for sociological research. In 1991, the U.S. Senate voted to forbid funding any survey on adult sexual practices. Nevertheless, a group of researchers was able to raise $1.6 million in private funding to develop the National Health and Social Life Survey (NHSLS). The NHSLS researchers argue that using data from their survey allows us to more easily address public policy issues such as AIDS, sexual harassment, welfare reform, sex discrimination, abortion, teenage pregnancy, and family planning.

KEY TERMS

Briefly define or identify the following terms in the spaces provided below. The definitions of these terms can be found later in this chapter of the study guide.

Scientific method	Correlation
Operational definition	Sample
Hypothesis	Random sample
Variable	Validity
Independent variable	Reliability
Dependent variable	Control variable
Causal logic	Research design

Survey	Hawthorne effect
Interview	Secondary analysis
Questionnaire	Content analysis
Quantitative research	Code of ethics
Qualitative research	Value neutrality
Observation	Percentage
Ethnography	Mean
Experiment	Mode
Experimental group	Median
Control group	Cross-tabulation

SELF-TEST

MODIFIED TRUE/FALSE QUESTIONS: If the statement below is true, write "true" in the space provided. If the statement is false, briefly correct the error.

1. The second step in the scientific method is formulating the hypothesis.

2. The dependent variable in a hypothesis is thought to cause or influence the independent variable.

3. Television viewers and radio listeners who e-mail their views on news headlines or on political contests are participating in a random sample.

4. After collecting and analyzing data, the researchers come to the final step in the scientific method: creating a theory.

5. Sociologists classify the Gallup poll and the Harris poll as examples of observation research.

6. There are two main types of samples: the interview and the questionnaire.

7. In William F. Whyte's *Street Corner Society*, he revealed his identity to the men he was studying and joined in their conversations, bowled with them, and participated in other leisure-time activities.

8.   The control group is exposed to an independent variable; the experimental group is not.

9.   Worker productivity in the Hawthorne studies diminished when researchers observed them, because the employees became self-conscious.

10.   The most frequently used existing sources in sociological research are census data, crime statistics, newspapers, and periodicals.

11.   The American Sociological Association's (ASA) Code of Ethics requires sociologists to maintain objectivity, preserve confidentiality, report all illegal behavior to appropriate authorities, and acknowledge research collaboration and assistance.

12.   Rik Scarce, a doctoral candidate in sociology, agreed to testify before a grand jury in 1993 and share with them research findings on his study of environmental protestors.

13.   Following the *Valdez* disaster, Exxon approached sociologists to do research on jury deliberations.

14.   Émile Durkheim's assertion that suicide was the result of social forces rather than supernatural forces was an illustration of a sociologist maintaining value neutrality.

15.   The development of computer technology has had little effect on sociological research.

MULTIPLE-CHOICE QUESTIONS: Read each question carefully and then select the best answer.

1.   The systematic, organized series of steps that ensures maximum objectivity and consistency in researching a problem is termed the
          a. dramaturgical approach.
          b. scientific method.
          c. functionalist approach.
          d. feminist view.

2.   The first step in any sociological research project is to
          a. collect data.
          b. define the problem.
          c. review previous research.
          d. formulate a hypothesis.

3.   An explanation of an abstract concept that is specific enough to allow a researcher to measure the concept is called a(n)
          a. hypothesis.
          b. operational definition.
          c. correlation.
          d. variable.

4.   Formulating the hypothesis is the _____ step in the scientific method.
          a. first
          b. second
          c. third
          d. fourth

5. A measurable trait or characteristic that is subject to change under different conditions is referred to as a(n)
    a. operational definition.
    b. theory.
    c. hypothesis.
    d. variable.

6. Suppose that how well a student does on a test is determined by how much the student studies for it. In this example, studying for an exam is a(n)
    a. correlation.
    b. independent variable.
    c. dependent variable.
    d. sample.

7. A correlation exists when
    a. one variable causes something to occur in another variable.
    b. two or more variables are causally related.
    c. a change in one variable coincides with a change in another variable.
    d. a negative relationship exists between two variables.

8. Through which type of research technique does a sociologist ensure that data are statistically representative of the population being studied?
    a. sampling
    b. experiments
    c. validity
    d. control variables

9. Which kind of sample is most frequently used by social scientists?
    a. a purposive sample
    b. a haphazard sample
    c. a random sample
    d. a nonscientific sample

10.   In order to obtain a random sample, a researcher might
       a.   administer a questionnaire to every fifth woman who enters a business office.
       b.   examine the attitudes of residents of a city by interviewing every twentieth name in the city's telephone book.
       c.   study the attitudes of registered Democratic voters by choosing every tenth name found on a city's list of registered Democrats.
       d.   do all of the above

11.   Which type of variable is a factor held constant to test the relative impact of the independent variable?
       a.   a control variable
       b.   an independent variable
       c.   a dependent variable
       d.   a hypothetical variable

12.   One reason that face-to-face interviews in the home are appropriate for social research in Baghdad is that
       a.   they help respondents to feel at ease.
       b.   they allow women to participate.
       c.   they are less expensive than written surveys.
       d.   a and b

13.   A detailed plan or method for obtaining data scientifically is called a(n)
       a.   sample.
       b.   experiment.
       c.   research design.
       d.   scientific method.

14.   A study that is generally in the form of an interview or a questionnaire is known as a(n)
       a.   observation.
       b.   ethnography.
       c.   experiment.
       d.   survey.

15.   A researcher can obtain a higher response rate by using which type of survey?
       a.   interviews
       b.   questionnaires
       c.   representative samples
       d.   observation techniques

16.   William F. Whyte's study of a low-income Italian neighborhood in Boston was a classic example of
       a.   participant observation research.
       b.   a survey.
       c.   content analysis.
       d.   an experiment.

17.   When sociologists want to study a possible cause-and-effect relationship, they may engage in what kind of research technique?
       a.   ethnography
       b.   survey research
       c.   secondary analysis
       d.   experimental research

18.   Which of the following is exposed to an independent variable?
       a.   the control group
       b.   the representative group
       c.   the experimental group
       d.   none of the above

19.   An instructor wants to determine if giving essay tests increases student learning. In one class that the instructor teaches, she continues to test as she has always done. In another class, she gives the students essay questions. She then measures the differences in learning, if any, between the two classes. The class that is given essay questions is the
       a.   control group.
       b.   representative group.
       c.   experimental group.
       d.   correlation group.

20. Subjects of observational research who deviate from their typical behavior because they realize that they are under observation are demonstrating
     a. the Hawthorne effect.
     b. causal logic.
     c. secondary analysis.
     d. none of the above

21. A researcher examines the literature written by Black novelists during the "Negro Renaissance" (1913–1935) to see if it reflects the political movements going on in the Black community in the United States at that time. What type of research methodology is being used in this example?
     a. an experiment
     b. interviews
     c. observation
     d. content analysis

22. Which of the following statements is NOT part of the Code of Ethics developed by the American Sociological Association?
     a. Acknowledge research collaboration and assistance.
     b. Preserve confidentiality.
     c. Protect subjects from personal harm.
     d. Make all research notes available for public scrutiny.

23. Max Weber
     a. recognized that it is impossible for scholars to prevent their personal values from influencing the questions that they select for research.
     b. stressed that researchers had to maintain the confidentiality of their subjects.
     c. emphasized that under no conditions could a researcher allow his or her personal feelings to influence the interpretation of data.
     d. both a and c

24.   Which of the following is a finding of the National Health and Social Life Survey?

    a.   Well-educated and affluent women are more likely to have abortions than poor teens.

    b.   Adults in the United States have sex 2-3 times per week.

    c.   Forty-seven percent of all women reported that they had been coerced into a sexual encounter at some time.

    d.   Eleven percent of men and nine percent of women stated that they were homosexual or bisexual.

25.   Which of the following was NOT a procedure used by the National Health and Social Life Survey (NHSLS) to ensure the validity of its findings on human sexuality?

    a.   interviews conducted in person

    b.   participatory observation

    c.   confidential survey that included questions about sensitive subject matter

    d.   redundant questions at different times in different ways during the 90-minute interview

FILL-IN QUESTIONS: Fill in the blank spaces in the sentences below with the correct words. Where two or more words are required, there will be a corresponding number of blank spaces.

1.   Unlike the typical citizen, the sociologist has a commitment to use the _____ method in studying society.

2.   The scientific method includes the following steps: defining the problem, reviewing the _____, formulating the hypothesis, selecting the research design and then collecting and analyzing the data, and developing the conclusion.

3.   A hypothesis is a speculative statement about the relationship between two or more factors known as _____.

4.   In formulating a(n) _____, researchers generally must suggest how one aspect of human behavior influences or affects another.

5.   Consider this hypothesis: The more an individual eats, the more he or she weighs. In this hypothesis, how much a person eats is a(n) _____ variable.

6.   In order to obtain data scientifically, researchers need to select a research
_____.

7.   A(n) _____ is a study, generally in the form of an interview or
questionnaire, which provides sociologists with information concerning how
people think and act.

8.   If scientists were testing a new type of toothpaste in an experimental setting, they
would administer the toothpaste to a(n) _____ group, but not to a(n)
_____ group.

9.   A researcher using census data in a way that was unintended by the initial
collectors of that information would be an example of _____
_____.

10.   Researchers can avoid the _____ effect by conducting secondary
analysis.

11.   Using content analysis, _____ _____ conducted a
pioneering exploration of how advertisements in 1979 portrayed women as
inferior to men.

12.   The American Sociological Association's Code of _____ requires
sociologists to maintain objectivity and integrity in research and to preserve the
confidentiality of their subjects.

13.   Examining the efforts of the Exxon Corporation to solicit social science research
on jury deliberations allows us to explore _____ issues in research.

14.   As part of their commitment to _____ neutrality, investigators have an
ethical obligation to accept research findings even when the data run counter to
their own personal views or widely accepted beliefs.

15.   In her book *The Death of White Sociology*, _____ _____
called attention to the tendency of mainstream sociology to treat the lives of
African Americans as a social problem.

UNDERSTANDING SOCIAL POLICY: Each of the following questions is based on material that appears in the social policy section on "Studying Human Sexuality." Briefly answer each question in the space provided.

1.   What research has been done in regard to studying human sexuality?

2.   How does the issue of value neutrality relate to studying human sexuality?

3.   What attempts have been made to administer a national survey and how did the government respond?

DEFINITIONS OF KEY TERMS

Scientific method: A systematic, organized series of steps that ensures maximum objectivity and consistency in researching a problem.

Operational definition: An explanation of an abstract concept that is specific enough to allow a researcher to assess the concept.

Hypothesis: A speculative statement about the relationship between two or more variables.

Variable: A measurable trait or characteristic that is subject to change under different conditions.

Independent variable: The variable in a causal relationship that causes or influences a change in a second variable.

Dependent variable: The variable in a causal relationship that is subject to the influence of another variable.

Causal logic: The relationship between a condition or variable and a particular consequence, with one event leading to the other.

Correlation: A relationship between two variables in which a change in one coincides with a change in the other.

Sample: A selection from a larger population that is statistically representative of that population.

Random sample: A sample for which every member of an entire population has the same chance of being selected.

Validity: The degree to which a measure or scale truly reflects the phenomenon under study.

Reliability: The extent to which a measure produces consistent results.

Control variable: A factor that is held constant to test the relative impact of an independent variable.

Research design: A detailed plan or method for obtaining data scientifically.

Survey: A study, generally in the form of an interview or questionnaire, that provides researchers with information about how people think and act.

Interview: A face-to-face or telephone questioning of a respondent to obtain desired information.

Questionnaire: A printed or written form used to obtain information from a respondent.

Quantitative research: Research that collects and reports data primarily in numerical form.

Qualitative research: Research that relies on what is seen in field or naturalistic settings more than on statistical data.

Observation: A research technique in which an investigator collects information through direct participation and/or by closely watching a group or community.

Ethnography: The study of an entire social setting through extended systematic observation.

Experiment: An artificially created situation that allows a researcher to manipulate variables.

Experimental group: The subjects in an experiment who are exposed to an independent variable introduced by a researcher.

Control group: The subjects in an experiment who are not introduced to the independent variable by the researcher.

Hawthorne effect: The unintended influence that observers of experiments can have on their subjects.

Secondary analysis: A variety of research techniques that make use of previously collected and publicly accessible information and data.

Content analysis: The systematic coding and objective recording of data, guided by some rationale.

Code of ethics: The standards of acceptable behavior developed by and for members of a profession.

Value neutrality: Max Weber's term for objectivity of sociologists in the interpretation of data.

Percentage: A portion of 100.

Mean: A number calculated by adding a series of values and then dividing by the number of values.

Mode: The single most common value in a series of values.

Median: The midpoint or number that divides a series of values into two groups of equal numbers of values.

Cross-tabulation: A table that shows the relationship between two or more variables.

ANSWERS TO SELF-TEST

Modified True/False Questions

1. The second step in the scientific method is reviewing the literature. Formulating the hypothesis is the third step in the process.

2. The variable hypothesized to cause or influence another is called the independent variable. The dependent variable "depends" on the influence of the independent variable.

3. The results of such polls reflect nothing more than the views of those who happened to see the television program or hear the radio broadcast and took the time, perhaps at some cost, to register their opinions.

4. After collecting and analyzing data, the researchers come to the final step in the scientific method: They develop the conclusion.

5. The Gallup poll and the Harris poll are among the best-known surveys of opinions in the United States.

6. There are two main types of *surveys*: the interview and the questionnaire.

7. True

8. The experimental group is exposed to an independent variable; the control group is not.

9. In the Hawthorne study, worker productivity increased because of the greater attention being paid to them and the novelty of being subjects in an experiment.

10. The most frequently used existing sources in sociological research are census data; crime statistics; and birth, death, marriage, divorce, and health statistics.

11. The Code of Ethics does not expect researchers to report all illegal behavior to appropriate authorities. This would be a violation of confidentiality, and would destroy the relationship the researcher has with the subject(s).

12. Rik Scarce declined to tell a federal grand jury what he knew, or even whether he knew anything, about a 1991 raid on a university research library. He was jailed for contempt of court and served 159 days in jail.

13. True

14. True

15. The development of computer technology has had a significant impact on sociological research. For example, sociologists can now handle larger and larger data sets.

Multiple-Choice Questions

1. b	10. c	19. c
2. b	11. a	20. a
3. b	12. d	21. d
4. c	13. c	22. d
5. d	14. d	23. d
6. b	15. a	24. a
7. c	16. a	25. b
8. a	17. d	
9. c	18. c	

Fill-In Questions

1. scientific	9. secondary analysis
2. literature	10. Hawthorne
3. variables	11. Erving Goffman
4. hypothesis	12. Ethics
5. independent	13. ethical
6. design	14. value
7. survey	15. Joyce Ladner
8. experimental; control	

Understanding Social Policy: Studying Human Sexuality

1. Sociologists have little reliable data on patterns of sexual behavior in the United States. Until recently, the only comprehensive study of sexual behavior was the famous two-volume Kinsey Report prepared in the 1940s. The volunteers interviewed for the report were not representative of the nation's adult population. In part, we lack reliable data on patterns of sexual behavior because it is difficult for researchers to obtain accurate information about this sensitive subject. Moreover, until AIDS emerged in the 1980s, there was little scientific demand for data on sexual behavior, except for specific concerns such as contraception.

2. The controversy surrounding research on human sexual behavior raises the issue of value neutrality, which becomes especially delicate when one considers the relationship of sociology to the government. The federal government has become the major source of funding for sociological research. Yet Max Weber urged that

sociology remain an autonomous discipline and that it not become unduly influenced by any one segment of society.

3. In 1987, the National Institute of Child Health and Human Development sought proposals for a national survey of sexual behavior. However, in 1991, the U.S. Senate voted to forbid funding any survey on adult sexual practices.

CHAPTER 3 CULTURE

Culture and Society

Development of Culture around the World
Cultural Universals
Innovation
Globalization, Diffusion and Technology
Biological Bases of Culture

Elements of Culture
Language
Norms
Sanctions
Values

Global Culture War

Culture and the Dominant Ideology

CASE STUDY: Culture at Wal-Mart

Cultural Variation
Aspects of Cultural Variation
Attitudes toward Cultural Variation

Social Policy and Culture: Bilingualism
The Issue
The Setting
Sociological Insights
Policy Initiatives

BOXES
SOCIOLOGY IN THE GLOBAL COMMUNITY: *Life in the Global Village*
SOCIOLOGY IN THE GLOBAL COMMUNITY: *Cultural Survival in Brazil*
SOCIOLOGY ON CAMPUS: *A Culture of Cheating?*

KEY POINTS

Culture and Society: **Culture** is the totality of learned, socially transmitted customs, knowledge, material objects, and behavior. It includes the ideas, values, and artifacts (for example, DVDs, comic books, and birth control devices) of groups of people. A large number of people are said to constitute a **society** when they live in the same territory, are relatively independent of people outside their area, and participate in a common culture. Members of a society generally share a common language, which facilitates day-to-day exchanges with others.

Cultural Universals: Despite their differences, all societies have developed certain common practices and beliefs, known as **cultural universals**. Anthropologist George Murdock compiled a list of cultural universals, including athletic sports, cooking, funeral ceremonies, medicine, marriage, and sexual restrictions. The cultural practices Murdock listed may be universal, but the manner in which they are expressed varies from culture to culture.

Material and Nonmaterial Culture: Sociologist William F. Ogburn made a useful distinction between the elements of material and nonmaterial culture. **Material culture** refers to the physical or technological aspects of our daily lives, including food, houses, factories, and raw materials. **Nonmaterial culture** refers to ways of using material objects and to customs, beliefs, philosophies, governments, and patterns of communication. Generally, the nonmaterial culture is more resistant to change than the material culture.

Biological Bases of Culture: **Sociobiology** is the systematic study of how biology affects human social behavior. Sociobiologists apply Charles Darwin's principle of natural selection to the study of human behavior. In its extreme form, sociobiology suggests that *all* behavior is the result of genetic or biological factors and that social interactions play no role in shaping people's conduct.

Language: **Language** is an abstract system of word meanings and symbols for all aspects of culture. It includes speech, written characters, numerals, symbols, and gestures and expressions of nonverbal communication. While language is a cultural universal, there are striking differences in the way different cultures use language.

Norms: **Norms** are the established standards of behavior maintained by a society. **Formal norms** generally have been written down and specify strict punishments for violators. By contrast, **informal norms** are generally understood, but are not precisely recorded. **Mores** are norms deemed highly necessary to the welfare of a society, often because they embody the most cherished principles of a people. **Folkways** are norms governing everyday behavior. Society is less likely to formalize folkways than mores, and their violation raises comparatively little concern.

Sanctions: **Sanctions** are penalties and rewards for conduct concerning a social norm. Conformity to a norm can lead to positive sanctions such as a pay raise, a medal, a word of gratitude, or a pat on the back. Negative sanctions include fines, threats, imprisonment, and stares of contempt.

Values: **Values** are collective conceptions of what is considered good, desirable, and proper—or bad, undesirable, and improper—in a culture. Values influence people's behavior and serve as criteria for evaluating the actions of others. The values, norms, and sanctions of a culture are often directly related.

Culture and the Dominant Ideology: Functionalists maintain that stability requires a consensus and the support of society's members; strong central values and common norms provide that support. Conflict theorists agree that a common culture may exist, but they argue that it serves to maintain the privileges of some groups rather than others. The term **dominant ideology** describes the set of cultural beliefs and practices that help to maintain powerful social, economic, and political interests. From a conflict perspective, the dominant ideology has major social significance. Not only do a society's most powerful groups and institutions control wealth and property; more importantly, they control the means of producing beliefs about reality through religion, education, and the media.

Subcultures: A **subculture** is a segment of society that shares a distinctive pattern of mores, folkways, and values that differs from the patterns of the larger society. The existence of many subcultures is characteristic of complex societies such as the United States. Members of a subculture participate in the dominant culture while at the same time engaging in their unique and distinctive forms of behavior. Frequently, a subculture will develop an **argot**, or specialized language, that distinguishes it from the wider society.

Culture Shock: Anyone who feels disoriented, uncertain, out of place, even fearful, when immersed in an unfamiliar culture may be experiencing **culture shock**. All of us, to some extent, take for granted the cultural practices of our society. As a result, it can be surprising and even disturbing to realize that other cultures do not follow our way of life.

Ethnocentrism: Sociologist William Graham Sumner coined the term **ethnocentrism** to refer to the tendency to assume that one's own culture and way of life represent the norm or are superior to all others. The ethnocentric person sees his or her own group as the center or defining point of culture and views all other cultures as deviations from what is "normal." Conflict theorists point out that ethnocentric value judgments serve to devalue groups and to deny equal opportunities. Functionalists note that ethnocentrism serves to maintain a sense of solidarity by promoting group pride.

Cultural Relativism: While ethnocentrism evaluates foreign cultures using the familiar culture of the observer as a standard of correct behavior, **cultural relativism** views people's behavior from the perspective of their own culture. It places a priority on understanding other cultures, rather than dismissing them as "strange" or "exotic." Unlike ethnocentrism, cultural relativism employs the kind of value neutrality in scientific study that Max Weber saw as so important.

Bilingualism: Bilingualism refers to the use of two or more languages in a particular setting, such as the workplace or schoolroom. This issue has prompted a great deal of debate among educators and policymakers. For a long time, people in the United States demanded conformity to a single language. Recent decades have seen challenges to this pattern of forced obedience to the dominant ideology. Beginning in the 1960s, active movements for Black pride and ethnic pride insisted that people regard the traditions of all race and ethnic subcultures as legitimate and important.

KEY TERMS

Briefly define or identify the following terms in the spaces provided below. The definitions of these terms can be found later in this chapter of the study guide.

Culture	Invention
Society	Diffusion
Culture industry	Technology
Cultural universal	Material culture
Innovation	Nonmaterial culture
Discovery	Culture lag

Sociobiology	Value
Language	Dominant ideology
Sapir-Whorf hypothesis	Culture war
Norm	Subculture
Formal norm	Argot
Law	Counterculture
Informal norm	Culture shock
Mores	Ethnocentrism
Folkway	Cultural relativism
Sanction	Bilingualism

SELF-TEST

MODIFIED TRUE/FALSE QUESTIONS: If the statement below is true, write "true" in the space provided. If the statement is false, briefly correct the error.

1.   In the view of sociologists, a portrait by Rembrandt is an aspect of culture; the work of graffiti artists is not.

2.   Some of the examples of cultural universals noted in your text are athletic sports, funerals, medicine, and war.

3.   There are two forms of innovation: discovery and diffusion.

4.   Material culture is more resistant to change than nonmaterial culture.

5.   A sociobiologist would argue that cultural similarities across societies are probably coincidental.

6.   The Sapir-Whorf hypothesis holds that language is a "given."

7.   The requirements for a college major and the rules of a card game are considered informal norms.

8.   Society is more likely to formalize mores than folkways.

9.   Even on clotheslines, mores in parts of Southeast Asia dictate male dominance in that women's attire is hung lower than that of men.

10.   Conformity to a norm can lead to positive sanctions.

11.   The values, norms, and sanctions of a culture are often directly related.

12.   From a functionalist perspective, the dominant ideology has major social significance. Not only do a society's most powerful groups and institutions control wealth and property; more importantly, they control the means of producing beliefs about reality through religion, education, and the family.

13.   Feminists would argue that the dominant ideology in the United States will help to control women and keep them in a subordinate position.

14.   Sociologist Robert Merton coined the term *ethnocentrism* to refer to the tendency to assume that one's own culture and way of life constitute the norm or are superior to all others.

15.   Cultural relativism requires that we accept without question every form of behavior characteristic of a culture.

MULTIPLE-CHOICE QUESTIONS: Read each question carefully and then select the best answer.

1.   Culture is defined as
     a.   the largest form of human group.
     b.   the totality of learned, socially transmitted customs, knowledge, material objects, and behavior.
     c.   the established standards of behavior maintained by a society.
     d.   norms governing everyday behavior.

2.   Which of the following is an aspect of culture?
     a.   a comic book
     b.   patriotic attachment to the flag of the United States
     c.   slang words
     d.   all of the above

3.   A list of cultural universals was compiled by anthropologist
     a.   Max Weber.
     b.   George Murdock.
     c.   Margaret Mead.
     d.   William F. Ogburn.

4.   The process by which a cultural item spreads from group to group or society to society is know as
     a.   innovation.
     b.   globalization.
     c.   diffusion.
     d.   culture lag

5.   The process of introducing a new idea or object to a culture is known as
     a.   innovation.
     b.   diffusion.
     c.   globalization.
     d.   cultural relativism.

6. The identification of a new moon of Saturn was an act of
    a. invention.
    b. discovery.
    c. diffusion.
    d. cultural integration.

7. The distinction between elements of material and nonmaterial culture was made by sociologist
    a. Max Weber.
    b. George Murdock.
    c. Margaret Mead.
    d. William F. Ogburn.

8. What term did William F. Ogburn introduce to refer to the period of maladjustment when the nonmaterial culture is still adapting to new material conditions?
    a. culture lag
    b. cultural relativism
    c. ethnocentrism
    d. diffusion

9. Sociobiologists apply this man's principle of natural selection to the study of social behavior.
    a. Herbert Spencer
    b. Charles Darwin
    c. Karl Marx
    d. William F. Ogburn

10. Which of the following is an example of language?
    a. hand gestures
    b. frowns and smiles
    c. written characters
    d. all of the above

11. The statement "Respect your elders" reflects which of the following?
    a. diffusion
    b. a cultural universal
    c. ethnocentrism
    d. a norm

12. In the United States, we often formalize norms into
    a. folkways.
    b. mores.
    c. values.
    d. laws.

13. Which of the following statements about norms is correct?
    a. People do not follow norms in all situations. In some cases, they evade a norm because they know it is weakly enforced.
    b. In some instances, behavior that appears to violate society's norms may actually represent adherence to the norms of a particular group.
    c. Norms are violated in some instances because one norm conflicts with another.
    d. all of the above

14. Health, love, and democracy are examples of
    a. mores.
    b. values.
    c. folkways.
    d. sanctions.

15. Which of the following statements about values is correct?
    a. Values never change.
    b. The values of a culture may change, but most remain relatively stable during any one person's lifetime.
    c. Values are constantly changing; sociologists view them as being very unstable.
    d. all of the above

16. Which theoretical perspective maintains that stability requires a consensus and the support of society's members?
    a. the conflict perspective
    b. the interactionist perspective
    c. social control theory
    d. the functionalist perspective

17.   Which sociological perspective argues that a common culture serves to maintain
        the privileges of some groups while keeping others in a subservient position?
        a.   the functionalist perspective
        b.   the conflict perspective
        c.   the interactionist perspective
        d.   all of the above

18.   Which of the following argued that a capitalist society has a dominant ideology
        that serves the interests of the ruling class?
        a.   Max Weber
        b.   Talcott Parsons
        c.   Karl Marx
        d.   Margaret Mead

19.   What term do sociologists use to refer to a segment of society that shares a
        distinctive pattern of mores, folkways, and values that differs from the pattern of
        the larger society?
        a.   dominant culture
        b.   counterculture
        c.   subculture
        d.   superculture

20.   Residents of a retirement community, workers on an offshore oil rig, and rodeo
        riders are all examples of what sociologists refer to as
        a.   subcultures.
        b.   countercultures.
        c.   cultural universals.
        d.   argot.

21.   Terrorist groups are examples of
        a.   cultural universals.
        b.   subcultures.
        c.   countercultures.
        d.   dominant ideologies.

22. While vacationing in Great Britain, you discover that the British drive on the "wrong" side of the road, are critical of your American accent, and will not accept dollars in stores. You feel disoriented and out of place. You are experiencing
    a. diffusion.
    b. the Hawthorne effect.
    c. the Sapir-Whorf hypothesis.
    d. culture shock.

23. Which sociological perspective emphasizes that ethnocentrism serves to maintain a sense of solidarity by promoting group pride?
    a. the functionalist perspective
    b. the conflict perspective
    c. the interactionist perspective
    d. the dramaturgical perspective

24. Evaluating the practices of other cultures on their basis of our own perspective is referred to as
    a. ethnocentrism.
    b. culture shock.
    c. cultural relativism.
    d. xenocentrism.

25. By 2006, how many states in the United States had declared English to be their official language?
    a. none
    b. 12
    c. 27
    d. 50

FILL-IN QUESTIONS: Fill in the blank spaces in the sentences below with the correct words. Where two or more words are required, there will be a corresponding number of blank spaces.

1. A(n) _____ is the largest form of human group.

2. The bow and arrow, the automobile, and the television are all examples of _____.

3. The emergence of Starbucks in China is an example of _____.

4.   Sociobiology is founded on the ideas of _____._____.

5.   Language does more than describe reality; it also serves to _____ the reality of a culture.

6.   "Put on some clean clothes for dinner" and "Thou shalt not kill" are both examples of _____ found in our culture.

7.   The United States has strong _____ against murder, treason, and child abuse that have been institutionalized into formal norms.

8.   As security searches in contemporary Iraq demonstrate, the sudden violation of long-standing cultural _____ can upset an entire population.

9.   During the 1980s and 1990s, there was growing support for values having to do with _____, power, and status.

10.   From a _____ perspective, the dominant ideology has major social significance. Not only do a society's most powerful groups and institutions control wealth and property; more importantly, they control the means of producing beliefs about reality through religion, education, and the media.

11.   Sociologists associated with the _____ perspective emphasize that language and symbols offer a powerful way for a subculture to maintain its identity.

12.   Hippies can be viewed as an example of a(n) _____.

13.   Countercultures are typically popular among the _____, who have the least investment in the existing culture.

14.   The _____ approach to social behavior points out that ethnocentric value judgments serve to devalue groups and contribute to denial of equal opportunities.

15.   Cultural relativism places a priority on _____ other cultures rather than dismissing them as "strange" or "exotic."

UNDERSTANDING SOCIAL POLICY: Each of the following questions is based on material that appears in the social policy section on "Bilingualism." Write a brief answer to each question in the space provided below.

1.   What is bilingualism?

2.   What is the functionalist view of bilingualism and what is the problem with this approach?

3.   What is the conflict view of bilingualism?

4.   What are the two major areas in which bilingualism has policy implications?

DEFINITIONS OF KEY TERMS

Culture: The totality of learned, socially transmitted customs, knowledge, material objects, and behavior.

Society: A fairly large number of people who live in the same territory, are relatively independent of people outside it, and participate in a common culture.

Culture industry: The worldwide media industry that standardizes the goods and services demanded by consumers

Cultural universal: A common practice or belief found in every culture.

Innovation: The process of introducing a new idea or object in a culture through discovery or invention.

Discovery: The process of making known or sharing the existence of an aspect of reality.

Invention: The combination of existing cultural items into a form that did not exist before.

Diffusion: The process by which a cultural item spreads from group to group or society to society.

Technology: Cultural information about how to use the material resources of the environment to satisfy human needs and desires.

Material culture: The physical or technological aspects of our daily lives.

Nonmaterial culture: Ways of using material objects, as well as customs, beliefs, philosophies, governments, and patterns of communication.

Culture lag: A period of maladjustment when the nonmaterial culture is still struggling to adapt to new material conditions.

Sociobiology: The systematic study of how biology affects human social behavior.

Language: An abstract system of word meanings and symbols for all aspects of culture; includes gestures and other nonverbal communication.

Sapir–Whorf hypothesis: A hypothesis concerning the role of language in shaping our interpretation of reality. It holds that language is culturally determined.

Norm: An established standard of behavior maintained by a society.

Formal norm: A norm that has been written down and that specifies strict punishments for violators.

Law: Governmental social control.

Informal norm: A norm that is generally understood but not precisely recorded.

Mores: Norms deemed highly necessary to the welfare of a society.

Folkway: A norm governing everyday behavior whose violation raises comparatively little concern.

Sanction: A penalty or reward for conduct concerning a social norm.

Value: A collective conception of what is considered good, desirable, and proper—or bad, undesirable, and improper—in a culture.

Dominant ideology: A set of cultural beliefs and practices that helps to maintain powerful social, economic, and political interests.

Culture war: The polarization of society over controversial cultural elements

Subculture: A segment of society that shares a distinctive pattern of mores, folkways, and values that differs from the pattern of the larger society.

Argot: Specialized language used by members of a group or subculture.

Counterculture: A subculture that deliberately opposes certain aspects of the larger culture.

Culture shock: The feeling of surprise and disorientation that people experience when they encounter cultural practices that are different from their own.

Ethnocentrism: The tendency to assume that one's culture and way of life represent the norm or are superior to all others.

Cultural relativism: The viewing of people's behavior from the perspective of their own culture.

Bilingualism: The use of two or more languages in a particular setting, such as the workplace or schoolroom, treating each language as equally legitimate.

ANSWERS TO SELF-TEST

Modified True/False Questions

1. Sociologists consider both a portrait by Rembrandt and the work of graffiti artists to be aspects of culture.

2. Athletic sports, funerals, and medicine are all on the list of cultural universals developed by George Murdock, but war is not.

3. There are two forms of innovation: discovery and invention.

4. Generally, nonmaterial culture is more resistant to change than is material culture.

5. A sociobiologist would argue that many cultural similarities are rooted in a common human genetic make-up.

6. The Sapir-Whorf hypothesis holds that language is not a "given." Rather, it is culturally determined.

7. The requirements for a college major and the rules of a card game are considered formal norms.

8. True

9. Even on clotheslines in parts of Southeast Asia, *folkways* dictate male dominance: women's attire is hung lower than that of men.

10. True

11. True

12. From a conflict perspective, the dominant ideology has major social significance. Not only do a society's most powerful groups and institutions control wealth and property; even more important, they control the means of producing beliefs about reality through religion, education, and the media.

13. True

14. Sociologist William Graham Sumner coined the term *ethnocentrism* to refer to the tendency to assume that one's own culture and way of life constitute the norm or are superior to all others.

15. While cultural relativism does not suggest that we must accept without question every form of behavior characteristic of a culture, it does require a serious and unbiased effort to evaluate norms, values, and customs in light of the distinctive culture of which they are a part.

Multiple-Choice Questions

1. b	10. d	19. c
2. d	11. d	20. a
3. b	12. d	21. c
4. c	13. d	22. d
5. a	14. b	23. a
6. b	15. b	24. a
7. d	16. d	25. c
8. a	17. b	
9. b	18. c	

Fill-In Questions

1. society	9. money
2. inventions	10. conflict
3. globalization	11. interactionist
4. Charles Darwin	12. counterculture
5. shape	13. young
6. norms	14. conflict
7. mores	15. understanding
8. norms	

Understanding Social Policy: Bilingualism

1. Bilingualism refers to the use of two or more languages in a particular setting, such as the workplace or schoolroom, treating each language as equally legitimate. Thus, a teacher of bilingual education may instruct children in their native language while gradually introducing them to the language of the host society. If the curriculum is also bicultural, it will teach children about the mores and folkways of both the dominant culture and the subculture.

2. For a long time, people in the United States demanded conformity to a single language. This demand coincides with the functionalist view that language serves to unify members of a society. In some cases, immigrant children were actually forbidden to speak their native languages on school grounds. There was little respect granted to immigrants' cultural traditions.

3. Conflict theory helps us to understand some of the attacks on bilingual programs. Many of the attacks stem from an ethnocentric point of view, which holds that any deviation from the majority is bad. This attitude tends to be expressed by those who wish to stamp out foreign influence wherever it occurs, especially in our schools.

4. Bilingualism has policy implications largely in two areas: efforts to maintain language purity and programs to enhance bilingual education. Nations vary dramatically in their tolerance for a variety of languages. Policymakers in the United States have been somewhat ambivalent in dealing with the issue of bilingualism. In 1965, the Elementary and Secondary Education Act (ESEA) provided for bilingual, bicultural education. Then, in the 1970s, the federal government took an active role in establishing the proper form for bilingual programs. However, more recently, federal policy has been less supportive of bilingualism, and local school districts have been forced to provide an increased share of funding for their bilingual programs.

CHAPTER

4 SOCIALIZATION AND THE LIFE COURSE

The Role of Socialization
> Social Environment: The Impact of Isolation
> The Influence of Heredity

The Self and Socialization
> Sociological Approaches to the Self
> Psychological Approaches to the Self

Agents of Socialization
> Family
> School
> Peer Group
> Mass Media and Technology
> Workplace
> Religion and the State

Socialization Throughout the Life Course
> The Life Course
> Anticipatory Socialization and Resocialization
> Role Transitions during the Life Course
>> The Sandwich Generation
>> Adjusting to Retirement

Social Policy and Socialization: Child Care around the World
> The Issue
> The Setting
> Sociological Insights
> Policy Initiatives

BOXES
> *SOCIOLOGY ON CAMPUS*: Impression Management by Students
> *TAKING SOCIOLOGY TO WORK*: Rakefet Avramovitz, Program Administrator, Child Care Law Center
> *SOCIOLOGY IN THE GLOBAL COMMUNITY*: Aging, Japanese Style

KEY POINTS

Socialization: **Socialization** is the process in which people learn the attitudes, values, and actions appropriate for members of a particular culture. From a microsociological perspective, socialization helps us discover how to behave "properly" and what to expect from others if we follow (or challenge) society's norms and values. From a macrosociological perspective, socialization provides for the transmission of a culture from one generation to the next, and thereby for the long-term continuance of a society.

Nature versus Nurture: Researchers have traditionally clashed over the relative importance of biological inheritance and environmental factors in human development; a conflict called the *nature versus nurture* (or *heredity versus environment*) debate. Today, most social scientists have moved beyond this debate, acknowledging instead the interaction of these variables in shaping human development.

Cooley and the Looking-Glass Self: In the early 1900s, Charles Horton Cooley advanced the belief that we learn who we are by interacting with others. Cooley used the phrase **looking-glass self** to emphasize that the self is the product of our social interactions with other people. A subtle but critical aspect of Cooley's looking-glass self is that the self results from an individual's "imagination" of how others view him or her.

Mead—Stages of the Self: George Herbert Mead continued Cooley's exploration of interactionist theory. Mead developed a useful model of the process by which the self emerges, defined by three distinct stages. During the preparatory stage, children merely imitate the people around them, especially family members with whom they continually interact. During the play stage, they begin to pretend to be other people. Just as an actor "becomes" a character, a child becomes a doctor, parent, superhero, or ship captain. Finally, in the game stage, the child of about eight or nine years old no longer just plays roles, but begins to consider several actual tasks and relationships simultaneously.

Goffman—Presentation of the Self: Early in life, the individual learns to slant his or her presentation of the self in order to create distinctive appearances and to satisfy particular audiences. Erving Goffman referred to this altering of the presentation of the self as **impression management**. He makes so many explicit parallels to the theater that his view has been termed the **dramaturgical approach**. According to this perspective, people resemble performers in action.

The Family as an Agent of Socialization: The family is the most important agent of socialization in the United States, especially for children. The lifelong process of socialization begins shortly after birth. Newborns are constantly orienting themselves to the outside world, and family members constitute an important part of their social environment. As the primary agents of socialization, parents play a critical role in guiding children into those gender roles deemed appropriate in a society.

Schools as an Agent of Socialization: Like the family, schools have an explicit mandate to socialize people in the United States—especially children—into the norms and values of our culture. Functionalists point out that schools, as agents of socialization, fulfill the function of teaching the values and customs of the larger society. Conflict theorists agree, but add that schools can reinforce the divisive aspects of society, especially those of social class.

Mass Media and Technology as Agents of Socialization: In the past 80 years, media innovations—radio, motion pictures, recorded music, television, and the Internet—have become important agents of socialization. Television and, increasingly, the Internet are critical forces in the socialization of children in the United States. One national study indicates that 68 percent of U.S. children have a television in their bedroom, and nearly half of all youths ages 8 to 18 use the Internet every day.

The Workplace as an Agent of Socialization: Learning to behave appropriately within an occupation is a fundamental aspect of human socialization. More and more young people work today. Some observers feel that the increasing numbers of teenagers working earlier in life and for longer hours are now finding the workplace almost as important an agent of socialization as school. Socialization in the workplace changes when it involves a more permanent shift from an after-school job to full-time employment.

The State and Religion as Agents of Socialization: Increasingly, social scientists are recognizing the importance of both government and religion as agents of socialization, because of their impact on the life course. Traditionally, family members have served as the primary caregivers in our culture, but in the twentieth century, the family's protective function was steadily transferred to outside agencies such as hospitals, mental health clinics, and insurance companies. Both government and organized religion have impacted the life course by reinstituting some of the rites of passage once observed in agricultural communities and early industrial societies.

Socialization Throughout the Life Course: Socialization is a lifelong process. As the members of a given society move through the life course the way in which they experience society changes. Personal preferences and circumstances affect the life course experience significantly, as do social factors such as class, race, and gender.

Anticipatory socialization refers to the processes of socialization in which a person "rehearses" for future positions, occupations, and social relationships. Occasionally, assuming a new social or occupational position requires us to unlearn a previous orientation. **Resocialization** refers to the process of discarding former behavior patterns and accepting new ones as part of a transition in one's life.

Total Institutions: Erving Goffman coined the term **total institution** to refer to an institution that regulates all aspects of a person's life under a single authority, such as a prison, the military, a mental hospital, or a convent. Because the total institution is generally cut off from the rest of society, it provides for all the needs of its members. People often lose their individuality within total institutions.

Adjusting to Retirement: Retirement is a rite of passage that marks a critical transition from one phase of a person's life to another. Retirement is not a single transition, but rather a series of adjustments that varies from one person to another. Like other aspects of life in the United States, the experience of retirement varies according to gender, race, and ethnicity.

Child Care around the World: Child care programs are not just babysitting services; they have an enormous influence on the development of young children. Researchers have found that high-quality child care centers do not adversely affect the socialization of children; in fact, good day care benefits children. Viewed from a conflict perspective, child care costs are an especially serious burden for lower class families. Feminists suggest that high-quality child care receives little governmental support because it is regarded as "merely a way to let women work."

KEY TERMS

Briefly define or identify the following terms in the spaces provided below. The definitions of these terms can be found later in this chapter of the study guide.

Socialization	Role taking
Personality	Generalized other
Self	Significant other
Looking-glass self	Impression management

Symbol	Dramaturgical approach
Face-work	Total institution
Cognitive theory of development	Degradation ceremony
Rite of passage	Midlife crisis
Life course approach	Sandwich generation
Anticipatory socialization	Gender role
Resocialization	

SELF-TEST

MODIFIED TRUE/FALSE QUESTIONS: If the statement below is true, write "true" in the space provided. If the statement is false, briefly correct the error.

1. Harry Harlow's study of Isabelle, who was raised in social isolation, supports the importance of socialization in development.

2. The self is a distinct identity that forms early in life and remains relatively unchanged as we age.

3. Charles Horton Cooley developed the concept of the looking-glass self.

4. Margaret Mead theorized about the development of the self in the early years of one's life.

5. During the preparatory stage identified by George Herbert Mead, children become skilled in role taking.

6. There appear to be striking differences in whom African Americans and Whites from similar economic backgrounds regard as their significant others.

7. Researchers are finding that families are socialized into multitasking as the social norm; devoting one's full attention to one task—even eating or driving—is less common on a typical day.

8. Sociologists Daniel Albas and Cheryl Albas found that students' impression management strategies are constrained by society's informal norms regarding modesty and consideration for less successful peers.

9. Conflict theorists emphasize that schools can reinforce the divisive aspects of society, especially those of social class.

10. Television is always a negative socializing influence.

11. Some observers feel that the increasing number of teenagers who are working earlier in life and for longer hours are now finding the workplace almost as important an agent of socialization as school.

12. The life course approach is distinctive because of its emphasis on events in infancy and early childhood.

13. Upon entering prison to begin "doing time," a person may experience the humiliation of a degradation ceremony as he or she is stripped of clothing, jewelry, and other personal possessions.

14. The state and religion have had a noteworthy impact on the life course by abolishing traditional rites of passage.

15. Since biological aging is the most important factor in how a person moves through the life course, social factors have little effect on how people experience transitions from one stage to the next.

MULTIPLE-CHOICE QUESTIONS: Read each question carefully and then select the best answer.

1. _____ is the lifelong process in which people learn the attitudes, values, and behaviors appropriate for members of a particular culture.
   a. Enculturation
   b. Socialization
   c. Personality formation
   d. Self-concept building

2. In everyday speech, the term _____ is used to refer to a person's typical patterns of attitudes, needs, characteristics, and behavior.
   a. enculturation
   b. socialization
   c. self-concept
   d. personality

3.　　Isabelle was
　　　a.　reared in an interracial family.
　　　b.　kept in almost total seclusion for the first six years of her life.
　　　c.　subjected to mistreatment in a mental institution.
　　　d.　a child whose language skills were of genius caliber.

4.　　Harry Harlow conducted a study of
　　　a.　Isabelle and the impact of social isolation on the socialization process.
　　　b.　Nell and the impact of social isolation on the socialization process.
　　　c.　rhesus monkeys that had been raised away from their mothers.
　　　d.　nature versus nurture that focused on sociobiology.

5.　　Which of the following used the phrase "looking-glass self" to emphasize that the self is the product of our social interactions with other people?
　　　a.　George Herbert Mead
　　　b.　Charles Horton Cooley
　　　c.　Erving Goffman
　　　d.　Harry Harlow

6.　　In which of Mead's stages of the self do children merely imitate the people around them?
　　　a.　the play stage
　　　b.　the game stage
　　　c.　the preparatory stage
　　　d.　the sensorimotor stage

7.　　Which of the following was among the first to analyze the relationship of symbols to socialization?
　　　a.　George Herbert Mead
　　　b.　Charles Horton Cooley
　　　c.　Erving Goffman
　　　d.　Sigmund Freud

8.　Which sociologist distinguished between significant others and generalized others?

    a.　George Herbert Mead

    b.　Charles Horton Cooley

    c.　Erving Goffman

    d.　W. I. Thomas

9.　Suppose a clerk tries to appear busier than he or she actually is when a supervisor happens to be watching. From which perspective would Goffman study this behavior?

    a.　the functionalist perspective

    b.　the conflict perspective

    c.　the psychological perspective

    d.　the interactionist perspective

10.　A person does poorly on a college chemistry test and later tells a friend, "The exam wasn't fair! There were trick questions, and it covered material that we weren't assigned!" This is an example of

    a.　reverse socialization.

    b.　face-work.

    c.　studied nonobservance.

    d.　anticipatory socialization.

11.　In studying the strategies that college students employ to create desired appearances after grades have been awarded, sociologists Daniel Albas and Cheryl Albas drew upon the concept of impression management developed by

    a.　George Herbert Mead.

    b.　Charles Horton Cooley.

    c.　Erving Goffman.

    d.　Jean Piaget.

12.　Jean Piaget found that although newborns have no self in the sense of a looking-glass image, they are quite

    a.　ethnocentric.

    b.　self-centered.

    c.　other-directed.

    d.　deterministic.

13.   According to Piaget, children begin to use words and symbols to distinguish objects and ideas during which stage in the development of thought processes?
    a.   the sensorimotor stage
    b.   the preoperational stage
    c.   the concrete operational stage
    d.   the formal operational stage

14.   The institution most closely associated with the process of socialization is the
    a.   family.
    b.   peer group.
    c.   school.
    d.   state.

15.   The term gender role refers to
    a.   the biological fact that we are male or female.
    b.   a role that is given to us by a teacher.
    c.   a role that is given to us in a play.
    d.   expectations regarding the proper behavior, attitudes, and activities of males and females.

16.   Which sociological perspective emphasizes that schools in the United States foster competition through built-in systems of reward and punishment?
    a.   the functionalist perspective
    b.   the conflict perspective
    c.   the interactionist perspective
    d.   the psychological perspective

17.   Television and the Internet are critical forces in the socialization of children in the United States. One national survey cited in the text found that nearly _____ percent of all youths ages 8 to 18 use the Internet every day.
    a.   25
    b.   35
    c.   50
    d.   75

18.   Which of the following is an example of a rite of passage?

   a.   school graduation

   b.   marriage

   c.   retirement

   d.   all of the above

19.   Assuming new social and occupational positions occasionally requires us to unlearn a previous orientation. We refer to this process as

   a.   anticipatory socialization.

   b.   socialization.

   c.   resocialization.

   d.   the life course.

20.   Which of the following is considered a total institution?

   a.   a university

   b.   a mental hospital

   c.   a factory

   d.   all of the above

21.   On the first day of basic training in the Army, a recruit has his civilian clothes replaced with army "greens," has his hair shaved off, loses his privacy, and finds that he must use a communal bathroom. All of these humiliating activities are part of

   a.   a significant other.

   b.   impression management.

   c.   a degradation ceremony.

   d.   face-work.

22.   Retirement is an example of

   a.   gerontocracy.

   b.   role fulfillment.

   c.   a rite of passage.

   d.   biological determinism.

23. A married couple with school-aged children also provides daily care for the husband's widowed father. This couple is an example of
    a. role fulfillment.
    b. a rite of passage.
    c. role strain.
    d. the sandwich generation.

24. Viewed from the _____ perspective, child care costs are an especially serious burden for lower-class families.
    a. functionalist
    b. conflict
    c. interactionist
    d. cognitive development

25. According to contemporary research,
    a. day care is physically damaging to children.
    b. day care adversely affects the socialization of children.
    c. good day care benefits children.
    d. none of the above

FILL-IN QUESTIONS: Fill in the blank spaces in the sentences below with the correct words. Where two or more words are required, there will be a corresponding number of blank spaces.

1. _____ provides for intergenerational transmission of culture, and it shapes the image that we hold of ourselves.

2. Studies of twins raised apart suggest that both _____ and _____ influence human development.

3. Those people who play a major role in shaping a person's identity, such as parents, friends, coworkers, coaches, and teachers, are _____ others.

4. A clerk may try to appear busier than he or she actually is if a supervisor happens to be watching. Sociologist _____ _____ examined such behavior using the dramaturgical approach.

5.   Early work in _____, such as that of Sigmund Freud, stressed the role of inborn drives—among them the drive for sexual gratification—in channeling human behavior.

6.   The first stage in Jean Piaget's well-known cognitive theory of development is the _____ stage, when children first discover that their hands are actually part of themselves.

7.   Traditional _____ roles include men being "tough" and women being "tender."

8.   The _____ perspective reminds us that socialization concerning not only masculinity and femininity, but also marriage and parenthood, begins in childhood as a part of family life.

9.   The _____ perspective of sociology emphasizes the role of schools in teaching the values and customs of the larger society.

10.   As children grow older, the family becomes less important in social development, while _____ _____ become more important.

11.   Among media innovations, television and the _____ are critical forces in the socialization of children.

12.   Both the government and organized religion have impacted the life course by reinstituting some of the _____ _____ _____ once observed in agricultural communities and early industrial societies.

13.   Preparation for many aspects of adult life begins with _____ socialization during childhood and adolescence, and continues throughout our lives as we prepare for new responsibilities.

14.   Resocialization is particularly effective when it occurs within a(n) _____ institution.

15.   Around age 40, men and women may experience a stress stemming from the realization that they may not have time to accomplish basic goals. This is called the _____ _____.

UNDERSTANDING SOCIAL POLICY: Each of the following questions is based on material that appears in the social policy section on "Child Care around the World." Write a brief answer to each question in the space provided below.

1.   According to studies, what is the effect of day care on children?

2.   What are the conflict and feminist concerns about day care?

3.   Why is the turnover of teaching personnel so high in day care centers?

DEFINITIONS OF KEY TERMS

Socialization: The lifelong process in which people learn the attitudes, values, and behaviors appropriate for members of a particular culture.

Personality: A person's typical patterns of attitudes, needs, characteristics, and behavior.

Self: A distinct identity that sets us apart from others.

Looking-glass self: A concept that emphasizes the self as the product of our social interactions with others.

Symbol: A gesture, object, or word that forms the basis of human communication.

Role taking: The process of mentally assuming the perspective of another and responding from that imagined viewpoint.

Generalized other: The attitudes, viewpoints, and expectations of society as a whole that a child takes into account in his or her behavior.

Significant other: An individual who is most important in the development of the self, such a parent, friend, or teacher.

Impression management: The altering of the presentation of the self in order to create distinctive appearances and satisfy particular audiences.

Dramaturgical approach: A view of social interaction in which people are seen as theatrical performers.

Face-work: The efforts people make to maintain the proper image and avoid public embarrassment.

Cognitive theory of development: The theory that children's thought progresses through four stages of development.

Rite of passage: A ritual marking the symbolic transition from one social position to another.

Life course approach: A research orientation in which sociologists and other social scientists look closely at the social factors that influence people throughout their lives, from birth to death.

Anticipatory socialization: Processes of socialization in which a person "rehearses" for future positions, occupations, and social relationships.

Resocialization: The process of discarding former behavior patterns and accepting new ones as part of a transition in one's life.

Total institution: An institution that regulates all aspects of a person's life under a single authority, such as a prison, the military, a mental hospital, or a convent.

Degradation ceremony: An aspect of the socialization process within some total institutions, in which people are subjected to humiliating rituals.

Midlife Crisis: A stressful period of self-evaluation that begins at about age 40.

Sandwich generation: The generation of adults who simultaneously try to meet the needs of both their parents and their children.

Gender role: Expectations regarding the proper behavior, attitudes, and activities of males and females.

ANSWERS TO SELF-TEST

Modified True/False Questions

1. Harry Harlow studied social isolation using rhesus monkeys.
2. The self continues to develop and change throughout our lives.
3. True
4. George Herbert Mead (no relation to Margaret Mead) theorized about the development of the self in the early years of one's life.
5. During the preparatory stage identified by George Herbert Mead, children merely imitate the people around them. Role taking occurs during the play stage.
6. There appears to be little difference in whom African Americans and Whites from similar backgrounds regard as their significant others.
7. True
8. True
9. True
10. Television can be a positive socializing influence. It can introduce children to unfamiliar lifestyles and cultures.

11. True

12. Social scientists who take a life course approach look at social factors that influence people throughout their lives

13. True

14. Both the government and organized religion have had a noteworthy impact on the life course by reinstituting the rites of passage that had disappeared in agricultural societies and in periods of early industrialization.

15. Social factors such as class, race, ethnicity, and gender are important factors throughout the life course and in how people experience transitions from one stage to the next.

Multiple-Choice Questions

1. b	10. b	19. c
2. d	11. c	20. b
3. b	12. b	21. c
4. c	13. b	22. c
5. b	14. a	23. d
6. c	15. d	24. b
7. a	16. b	25. c
8. a	17. c	
9. d	18. d	

Fill-In Questions

1. Socialization	9. functionalist
2. heredity; environment	10. peer groups
3. significant	11. Internet
4. Erving Goffman	12. anticipatory
5. psychology	13. total
6. sensorimotor	14. midlife crisis
7. gender	15. rites of passage
8. interactionist	

Understanding Social Policy: Child Care around the World

1. Studies indicate that the socialization of children placed in high-quality day care centers is not adversely affected by such experiences; in fact, good day care benefits children. It is difficult, however, to generalize about child care, since there is so much variability among day care providers.

2. Conflict theorists and feminists are concerned that parents in wealthy neighborhoods have an easier time finding day care than those in poor or working-class communities, that day care costs are an especially serious burden for lower-class families, and that nearly all day care workers are women who often find themselves in low-status, minimum-wage jobs.

3. Nearly all child care workers are women; many find themselves in low-status, minimum-wage jobs. Half of the child care workers in the U.S. earn less than $8.70 per hour, which is typically less than food servers, messengers, and gas station attendants make.

5 SOCIAL INTERACTION, GROUPS, AND SOCIAL STRUCTURE

Social Interaction and Reality

Elements of Social Structure
   Statuses
   Social Roles
   Groups
   Social Networks
   Virtual Worlds
   Social Institutions

Understanding Organizations
   Formal Organizations and
     Bureaucracies
   Characteristics of a Bureaucracy
   Bureaucracy and Organizational
     Culture

Social Structure in Global Perspective
   Durkheim's Mechanical and
     Organic Solidarity
   Tönnies's Gemeinschaft and
     Gesellschaft
   Lenski's Sociocultural Evolution
     Approach

Social Policy and Social Interaction:
Regulating the Net
   The Issue
   The Setting
   Sociological Insights
   Policy Initiatives

BOXES
   RESEARCH TODAY: *Disability as a Master Status*
   SOCIOLOGY IN THE GLOBAL COMMUNITY: *McDonald's and the Worldwide Bureaucratization of Society*

KEY POINTS

Social Interaction and Social Structure: Sociologists use the term **social interaction** to refer to the ways in which people respond to one another. **Social structure** refers to the way in which a society is organized into predictable relationships. These concepts are central to sociological study.

Social Interaction and Reality: According to Herbert Blumer, reality is shaped by our perceptions, evaluations, and definitions. The ability to define social reality reflects a group's power within a society. Indeed, one of the most crucial aspects of the relationship between dominant and subordinate groups is the ability of the dominant or majority group to define a society's values.

Statuses: We normally think of a person's "status" as having to do with influence, wealth, and fame. However, sociologists use the term **status** to refer to any of the full range of socially defined positions within a large group or society, from the lowest to the highest position. Clearly, a person can hold a number of statuses at the same time.

Ascribed and Achieved Status: An **ascribed status** is assigned to a person by society without regard to that person's unique talents or characteristics. Generally, this assignment takes place at birth; thus, a person's racial background, gender, and age are all considered ascribed statuses. Unlike ascribed statuses, an **achieved status** comes to us largely through our own efforts. We must do something, such as going to school, learning a skill, establishing a friendship, or inventing a new product, in order to acquire an achieved status.

Social Roles: A **social role** is a set of expectations for people who occupy a given social position or status. With each distinctive social status—whether ascribed or achieved— come particular role expectations. Roles are a significant component of social structure. Viewed from a functionalist perspective, roles contribute to a society's stability by enabling members to anticipate the behavior of others and to pattern their own actions accordingly. Yet, social roles can also be dysfunctional if they restrict people's interaction and relationships.

Groups: In sociological terms, a **group** is any number of people with similar norms, values, and expectations who interact with one another on a regular basis. Groups play a vital part in a society's social structure. Much of our social interaction takes place within groups and is influenced by their norms and sanctions.

Primary and Secondary Groups: Sociologist Charles Horton Cooley coined the term **primary group** to refer to a small group characterized by intimate, face-to-face association and cooperation. When we find ourselves identifying closely with a group, it is probably a primary group. However, we also participate in many groups that are not characterized by close bonds of friendship, such as large classes and business associations. The term **secondary group** refers to a formal, impersonal group in which there is little social intimacy or mutual understanding.

In-Groups, Out-Groups, and Reference Groups: An **in-group** is a group or category to which people feel they belong, and an **out-group** is a group or category to which people feel they do not belong. Sociologists use the term **reference group** when speaking of any group that individuals use as a standard for evaluating themselves and their own behavior. Reference groups have two basic purposes: (1) They serve a normative function by setting and enforcing standards of conduct and belief, and (2) they also perform a comparison function by serving as a standard against which people can measure themselves and others.

Social Institutions: The mass media, the government, the economy, the family, and the health care system are all examples of social institutions found in our society. **Social institutions** are organized patterns of beliefs and behavior centered on basic social needs, such as replacing personnel (the family) and preserving order (the government).

Functionalist View of Social Institutions: One way to understand social institutions is to see how they fulfill essential functions. Social scientists have identified five major tasks, or functional prerequisites, that a society or a relatively permanent group must accomplish if it is to survive. These are (1) replacing personnel, (2) teaching new recruits, (3) producing and distributing goods and services, (4) preserving order, and (5) providing and maintaining a sense of purpose.

Conflict View of Social Institutions: While both the functionalist and the conflict perspectives agree that social institutions are organized to meet basic social needs, conflict theorists object to the implication inherent in the functionalist view that the outcome is necessarily efficient and desirable. From a conflict perspective, major institutions help maintain the privileges of the most powerful individuals and groups within a society, while contributing to the powerlessness of others. Conflict theorists, as well as feminists and interactionists, have pointed out that social institutions also operate in gendered or racist environments. In schools, offices, and government institutions, assumptions that are made about what people can do reflect the sexism and racism of the larger society.

Interactionist View of Social Institutions: Interactionist theorists emphasize that our social behavior is conditioned by the roles and statuses that we accept, the groups to which we belong, and the institutions within which we function.

Formal Organizations: As contemporary societies have shifted to more advanced forms of technology and their social structures have become more complex, our lives have become increasingly dominated by large secondary groups referred to as **formal organizations**. A formal organization is a group designed for a special purpose and structured for maximum efficiency. The U.S. Postal Service, the Boston Pops orchestra, and the college you attend are all examples of formal organizations. In our society, formal organizations fulfill an enormous variety of personal and societal needs and shape the lives of every one of us.

Characteristics of a Bureaucracy: A **bureaucracy** is a component of formal organization that uses rules and hierarchical ranking to achieve efficiency. Elements of bureaucracy enter into almost every occupation in an industrial society. Max Weber first directed researchers to the significance of bureaucratic structure. For analytical purposes, he developed an ideal type of bureaucracy that would reflect the most characteristic aspects of all human organizations. He argued that the ideal bureaucracy will have five basic characteristics: division of labor, hierarchy of authority, written rules and regulations, impersonality, and employment based on technical qualifications.

Durkheim's Mechanical and Organic Solidarity: Émile Durkheim argued that social structure depends on the division of labor in a society. In a society in which there is a minimal division of labor, a collective consciousness develops that emphasizes group solidarity. Durkheim called this **mechanical solidarity**. As societies become more advanced technologically, a greater division of labor takes place. These societies are characterized by **organic solidarity**, a collective consciousness that rests on mutual interdependence.

Tönnies's *Gemeinschaft* and *Gesellschaft*: According to sociologist Ferdinand Tönnies, the ***Gemeinschaft*** community is typical of rural life. It is a small community in which people have similar backgrounds and life experiences. In contrast, the ***Gesellschaft*** is an ideal community that is characteristic of modern urban life. In this community, most people are strangers who feel little in common with other community residents. Self-interest dominates, and there is little consensus concerning values or commitment to the group.

Lenski's Sociocultural Evolution Approach: Sociologist Gerhard Lenski sees human societies as undergoing a process of change characterized by a dominant pattern known as **sociocultural evolution**. In Lenski's view, a society's level of technology is critical to the way it is organized. There are three types of preindustrial societies, which are categorized according to the way in which the economy is organized: (1) the hunting-and-gathering society, (2) the horticultural society, and (3) the agrarian society. As the industrial revolution proceeded, a new form of social structure emerged. An **industrial society** is a society that depends on mechanization to produce its goods and services. Industrial societies rely on new inventions that facilitate agricultural and industrial production, and on new sources of energy, such as steam. Since the 1970s sociologists have been studying societal changes that occur as societies shift from industrial to **postindustrial** societies characterized by the processing of services and information. Many sociologists now hold that technologically sophisticated societies are emerging as **postmodern** societies.

Bureaucratization as a Process: Sociologists have used the term bureaucratization to refer to the process by which a group, organization, or social movement becomes increasingly bureaucratic. Normally, we think of bureaucratization in terms of large organizations. But bureaucratization also takes place within small-group settings.

The Iron Law of Oligarchy: German sociologist Robert Michels studied socialist parties and labor unions in Europe before World War I and found that such organizations were becoming increasingly bureaucratic. Michels originated the idea of the **iron law of oligarchy**, under which a democratic organization will eventually develop into a bureaucracy ruled by a few. Michels argued that members of an oligarchy are strongly motivated to maintain their leadership roles, privileges, and power.

Bureaucracy and Organizational Culture: How does bureaucratization affect the average individual who works in an organization? According to the **classical theory** of formal organizations, also known as the **scientific management approach**, workers are motivated almost entirely by economic rewards. The **human relations approach** emphasizes the role of people, communication, and participation within a bureaucracy.

KEY TERMS

Briefly define or identify the following terms in the spaces provided below. The definitions of these terms can be found later in this chapter of the study guide.

Social interaction	Group
Social structure	Primary group
Status	Secondary group
Ascribed status	In-group
Achieved status	Out-group

Master status	Reference group
Social role	Coalition
Role conflict	Social network
Role strain	Avatar
Role exit	Social institution
Formal organization	Mechanical solidarity
Bureaucracy	Organic solidarity
Ideal type	*Gemeinschaft*
Alienation	*Gesellschaft*
Trained incapacity	Sociocultural evolution
Goal displacement	Technology
Peter principle	Hunting-and-gathering society

Bureaucratization	Horticultural society
McDonaldization	Agrarian society
Iron law of oligarchy	Industrial society
Classical theory of formal organizations	Postindustrial society
Scientific management approach	Postmodern society
Human relations approach	Net neutrality

SELF-TEST

MODIFIED TRUE/FALSE QUESTIONS: If the statement below is true, write "true" in the space provided. If the statement is false, briefly correct the error.

1. Friends talking on the telephone and co-workers communicating by computer are engaged in social interaction.

2. The four basic elements of social structure are functions, behaviors, statuses, and social roles.

3. It is relatively easy to change an ascribed status.

4.   With each distinctive social role, whether ascribed or achieved, come particular status expectations. However, actual performance varies from individual to individual.

5.   The last stage of role exit involves the creation of a new identity.

6.   Each of the following statements implies the existence of reference groups: "Our generation does not have those sexual hang-ups," "We Christians go to church every week," and "We Southerners have to stick together."

7.   Only one reference group can influence an individual at a given time.

8.   The concept of social networking is changing rapidly as people increasingly use email and Internet sites such as FaceBook.

9.   According to Talcott Parsons and Robert Merton, the five major tasks or functional prerequisites that a society or a relatively permanent group must accomplish if it is to survive are replacing personnel, teaching new recruits, producing and distributing goods and services, preserving order, and providing and maintaining a sense of purpose.

10.   The five characteristics of bureaucracies that Weber discussed include division of labor, hierarchy of authority, written rules and regulations, dysfunctions, and impersonality.

11.   Max Weber used the term goal displacement to refer to overzealous conformity to official regulations.

12.   Organic solidarity implies a group orientation in the community.

13.   Social change is an important aspect of life in the *Gemeinschaft*; it can be strikingly evident even within a single generation.

14.   The iron law of oligarchy describes how even a democratic organization will develop into a bureaucracy ruled by a few (the oligarchy).

15.   It was not until workers organized unions, and forced management to recognize that they were not objects, that theorists of formal organizations began to revise the classical approach.

MULTIPLE-CHOICE QUESTIONS: Read each question carefully and then select the best answer.

1.   In Zimbardo's mock prison experiment at Stanford University
    a.   the social interactions between the prisoners and the guards influenced the social structure of the prison.
    b.   the social structure of the prison influenced the social interactions between the prisoners and the guards.
    c.   there was no relationship between social interaction and social structure.
    d.   Zimbardo believed that social structure and social interaction influence each other.

2.   Which sociologist saw that the "definition of the situation" could mold the thinking and personality of the individual?
    a.   Philip Zimbardo
    b.   Herbert Blumer
    c.   William I. Thomas
    d.   Erving Goffman

3.   Which of the following is an ascribed status?
    a.   daughter
    b.   long-distance runner
    c.   doctor
    d.   all of the above

4.   Which of the following is an achieved status?
    a.   senior citizen
    b.   member of the female sex
    c.   bank robber
    d.   Native American

5.   Arthur Ashe was a retired tennis star, an author, a political activist, and a person with AIDS. If he is remembered mainly as a well-known personality with AIDS, then this is his
    a.   master status.
    b.   self-fulfilling prophecy.
    c.   ascribed status.
    d.   social role.

6.   During World War II, Christians living in Nazi Germany had to choose between trying to protect Jewish friends and associates or turning them in to the authorities. This is an example of
    a.   cultural universalism.
    b.   role strain.
    c.   functional prerequisites.
    d.   role conflict.

7. You are a student at XYZ College, and you have your sociology and history final exams on the same morning. You know that preparing for both exams at the same time is going to lead to lower grades in one or both of the exams. The conflict that you are experiencing as you try to fulfill both of your responsibilities at the college is an example of
    a. role conflict.
    b. role exit.
    c. role strain.
    d. role dissonance.

8. Which of the following would experience role exit?
    a. a retired person
    b. a recovering alcoholic
    c. a nun who leaves her religious order
    d. all of the above

9. In sociological terms, which of the following constitutes a group?
    a. members of a hospital's business office
    b. all residents of the state of Vermont
    c. women in the United States ages 50 years and older
    d. all of the above

10. Close friends who have known each other since childhood would be an example of a(n)
    a. primary group.
    b. secondary group.
    c. out-group.
    d. formal organization.

11. _____ groups often emerge in the workplace among those who share special understandings about their occupation.
    a. Primary
    b. Secondary
    c. Out-
    d. Formal

12. The purpose of a reference group is to serve a(n)
    a. normative function by enforcing standards of conduct and belief.
    b. comparison function by serving as a standard against which people can measure themselves and others.
    c. elimination function by dissolving groups that no longer have a social purpose.
    d. both a and b

13. Which of the following is NOT true of virtual worlds?
    a. Virtual worlds have become increasingly consumer oriented.
    b. Virtual life can migrate into real life.
    c. Virtual worlds have remained essentially apolitical.
    d. Virtual networks can help preserve real-life networks.

14. Which sociological perspective has identified five major tasks that a society must accomplish if it is to survive?
    a. the functionalist perspective
    b. the conflict perspective
    c. the interactionist perspective
    d. the clinical perspective

15. Which sociological perspective emphasizes that the outcome of major social institutions is not necessarily efficient and desirable?
    a. the functionalist perspective
    b. the conflict perspective
    c. the interactionist perspective
    d. all of the above

16. In studying the social behavior of word processors in a Chicago law firm, sociologist Mitchell Duneier drew on the
    a. functionalist perspective.
    b. conflict perspective.
    c. interactionist perspective.
    d. macrosociological perspective.

17.   Which pioneer of sociology first directed researchers to the significance of bureaucratic structure?
   a.   Émile Durkheim
   b.   Max Weber
   c.   Karl Marx
   d.   Ferdinand Tönnies

18.   The President of the United States need not be a good typist; a surgeon need not be able to fill a cavity. This is because of the bureaucratic characteristic of
   a.   division of labor.
   b.   impersonality.
   c.   employment based on technical qualifications.
   d.   written rules and regulations.

19.   Steve is the star of the college football team. He takes a history course and fails all of the exams in that course. Nevertheless, the instructor gives Steve an "A" in the course. This would violate which component of bureaucracies?
   a.   division of labor
   b.   written rules and regulations
   c.   employment based on technical qualifications
   d.   impersonality

20.   Claude is in a major automobile accident and is severely injured. When he is brought by ambulance to the hospital, he is refused admission because he cannot find his health insurance card. This situation would illustrate
   a.   the Peter principle.
   b.   trained incapacity.
   c.   goal displacement.
   d.   division of labor.

21.   When workers organized unions and forced management to recognize that they were not objects, theorists of formal organizations began to revise the
   a.   classical theory of formal organizations.
   b.   scientific management approach.
   c.   human relations approach.
   d.   both a and b

22.   The tendency for every employee in a bureaucracy to rise to her or his level of incompetence is
      a. bureaucratic ritualism.
      b. trained incapacity.
      c. Parkinson's Law.
      d. the Peter Principle.

23.   Daniel Bell describes postmodern society as basically consensual, with an open and competitive decision making that includes diverse organizations and interest groups that will result in greater overall stability.   This is a
      a. functionalist outlook.
      b. conflict theory outlook.
      c. feminist outlook.
      d. interactionist outlook.

24.   Gerhard Lenski's theory of sociocultural evolution, a society's level of _____ is critical to the way it is organized.
      a. agriculture
      b. health care
      c. technology
      d. all of the above

25.   Regular instant messaging to buddy list friends, activity in MySpace interest groups, and online impression management via screen names and avatars are especially interesting to
      a. functionalists.
      b. conflict theorists.
      c. interactionists.
      d. classical theorists.

FILL-IN QUESTIONS: Fill in the blank spaces in the sentences below with the correct words. Where two or more words are required, there will be a corresponding number of blank spaces.

1.   _____ theorists are especially interested in ascribed statuses, since these statuses often confer privileges or reflect a person's membership in a subordinate group.

2.   With each distinctive social status come particular _____ expectations.

3.   Contemporary sociologists have suggested that society has attached a
        _____ to many forms of disability and that this leads to prejudicial
        treatment.

4.   Sociologist Helen Rose Fuchs Ebaugh developed the term _____
        _____ to describe the process of disengagement from a role that is
        central to one's self-identity, and the reestablishment of an identity in a new role.

5.   When we find ourselves identifying closely with a group, it is probably a
        _____ group.

6.   In many cases, people model their behavior after groups to which they may not
        belong. These groups are called _____ groups.

7.   Finding new members is not enough. A group or society must also encourage
        recruits to learn and accept its values and customs. This can take place formally
        within schools (where learning is a _____ function) or informally,
        through interaction in peer groups (where instruction is a _____
        function).

8.   Viewed from a(n) _____ perspective, major social institutions help
        maintain the privileges of the most powerful individuals and groups in a society,
        while contributing to the powerlessness of others.

9.   According to Durkheim, societies with a minimal division of labor are
        characterized by _____ _____, while societies with a
        complex division of labor are characterized by _____
        _____.

10.   The concepts of *Gemeinschaft* and *Gesellschaft* were developed by German
        sociologist _____ _____.

11.   The theory of sociocultural evolution was developed by _____
        _____.

12.   _____ societies rely on new inventions that facilitate agricultural
        and industrial production, and on new sources of energy, such as steam.

13.   Max Weber developed a(n) _____ _____ of bureaucracy,
        which reflects the most characteristic aspects of all human organizations.

14. The division of labor in a bureaucracy can sometimes cause workers to become so specialized that they develop blind spots and fail to notice obvious problems. This problem is called _____ _____.

15. Lack of online privacy is one result of _____ _____, the principle that the government should allow the internet to be as unregulated as possible.

UNDERSTANDING SOCIAL POLICY: Each of the following questions is based on material that appears in the social policy section on "Regulating the Net." Write a brief answer to each question in the space provided below.

1. Describe the disparities in internet usage that concern conflict theorists. What are some consequences of lack of access that would concern conflict theorists?

2. Many teenagers and college students use the internet for confessional communications and photos that were unheard of even a decade ago. As this trend continues, what effects might there be on the concept of reasonable personal privacy and legal responses to the violation of privacy?

3. Describe some ways in which the internet is self-regulating.

DEFINITIONS OF KEY TERMS

Social interaction: The ways in which people respond to one another.

Social structure: The way in which a society is organized into predictable relationships.

Status: A term used by sociologists to refer to any of the full range of socially defined positions within a large group or society.

Ascribed status: A social position that is assigned to a person by society without regard for the person's unique talents or characteristics.

Achieved status: A social position a person attains largely through his or her own efforts.

Master status: A status that dominates others and thereby determines a person's general position in society.

Social role: A set of expectations for people who occupy a given social position or status.

Role conflict: The situation that occurs when incompatible expectations arise from two or more social positions held by the same person.

Role strain: The difficulty that arises when the same social position imposes conflicting demands and expectations.

Role exit: The process of disengagement from a role that is central to one's self-identity in order to establish a new role and identity.

Group: Any number of people with similar norms, values, and expectations who interact with one another on a regular basis.

Primary group: A small group characterized by intimate, face-to-face association and cooperation.

Secondary group: A formal, impersonal group in which there is little social intimacy or mutual understanding.

In-group: Any group or category to which people feel they belong.

Out-group: A group or category to which people feel they do not belong.

Reference group: Any group that individuals use as a standard for evaluating themselves and their own behavior.

Coalition: A temporary or permanent alliance geared toward a common goal.

Social network: A series of social relationships that links a person directly to others and through them indirectly to still more people.

Avatar: A three dimensional model, two dimensional icon, or constructed personality that is assumed by the user of an Internet site

Social institution: An organized pattern of beliefs and behavior centered on basic social needs.

Formal organization: A group designed for a special purpose and structured for maximum efficiency.

Bureaucracy: A component of formal organization that uses rules and hierarchical ranking to achieve efficiency.

Ideal type: A construct or model for evaluating specific cases.

Alienation: A condition of estrangement or dissociation from the surrounding society.

Trained incapacity: The tendency of workers in a bureaucracy to become so specialized that they develop blind spots and fail to notice obvious problems.

Goal displacement: Overzealous conformity to official regulations of a bureaucracy.

Peter principle: A principle of organizational life according to which every employee within a hierarchy tends to rise to his or her level of incompetence.

McDonaldization: The process by which the principles of the fast-food restaurant are coming to dominate more and more sectors of American society as well as the rest of the world.

Bureaucratization: The process by which a group, organization, or social movement becomes increasingly bureaucratic.

Iron law of oligarchy: A principle of organizational life under which even a democratic organization will develop into a bureaucracy ruled by a few individuals.

Classical theory: An approach to the study of formal organizations that views workers as being motivated almost entirely by economic rewards.

Scientific management approach: Another name for the classical theory of formal organizations.

Human relations approach: An approach to the study of formal organizations that emphasizes the role of people, communication, and participation in a bureaucracy, and tends to focus on the informal structure of the organization.

Mechanical solidarity: A collective consciousness that emphasizes group solidarity, characteristic of societies with minimal division of labor.

Organic solidarity: A collective consciousness that rests on mutual interdependence, characteristic of societies with a complex division of labor.

Gemeinschaft: A close-knit community, often found in rural areas, in which strong personal bonds unite members.

Gesellschaft: A community, often urban, that is large and impersonal, with little commitment to the group or consensus on values.

Sociocultural evolution: Long-term trends in societies resulting from the interplay of continuity, innovation, and selection.

Technology: Cultural information about how to use the material resources of the environment to satisfy human needs and desires.

Hunting-and-gathering society: A preindustrial society in which people rely on whatever foods and fibers are readily available in order to survive.

Horticultural society: A preindustrial society in which people plant seeds and crops rather than merely subsist on available foods.

Agrarian society: The most technologically advanced form of preindustrial society. Members are engaged primarily in the production of food, but increase their crop yields through technological innovations such as the plow.

Industrial society: A society that depends on mechanization to produce its goods and services.

Postindustrial society: A society whose economic system is engaged primarily in the processing and control of information.

Postmodern society: A technologically sophisticated society that is preoccupied with consumer goods and media images.

Net neutrality: The principle that the government should remain nonselective of neutral toward online content

ANSWERS TO SELF-TEST

Modified True/False Questions

1. True
2. The five basic elements of social structure are statuses, social roles, groups, social networks, and social institutions.
3. In many cases, there is little that people can do to change an ascribed status.
4. With each distinctive social status, whether ascribed or achieved, come particular role expectations.
5. True
6. Each of the phrases implies the existence of in-groups and out-groups—groups to which we feel that we belong or do not belong.
7. It is not uncommon for two or more reference groups to influence us at the same time.
8. True
9. The five major tasks or functional prerequisites were developed by David F. Aberle, Raymond Mack, and Calvin Bradford.
10. Dysfunctions are not one of the five characteristics of bureaucracy discussed by Max Weber. Employment based on technical qualifications should be added to the list.
11. Robert Merton used the term goal displacement to refer to overzealous conformity to official regulations.
12. Mechanical solidarity implies group orientation.
13. Social change is an important aspect of life in the *Gesellschaft*; it can be strikingly evident within a single generation.
14. True
15. True

Multiple-Choice Questions

1. b	10. a	19. c
2. c	11. b	20. c
3. a	12. d	21. a
4. c	13. c	22. d
5. a	14. a	23. a
6. d	15. b	24. c
7. c	16. c	25. c
8. d	17. b	
9. a	18. a	

Fill-In Questions

1. Conflict
2. role
3. stigma
4. role exit
5. primary
6. reference
7. manifest; latent
8. conflict
9. mechanical solidarity; organic solidarity
10. Ferdinand Tönnies
11. Gerhard Lenski
12. Industrial
13. functionalist
14. ideal type
15. net neutrality

Understanding Social Policy: Regulating the Net

1. People in low-income groups, rural residents, and people living in developing nations have less access to the internet and all of the resources it provides. As Internet access becomes more important in schooling, employment, commerce, and even areas such as medical care, people with poor access will be left further and further behind. Examples: Students may not be able to complete assignments, apply to college, find out about financial aid opportunities, etc.

2. As people become more used to sharing personal information, photos, etc., the concept of a right to personal privacy could erode. Those who have not had pre-Internet/camera phone levels of privacy may find it hard to value or miss what they have not had. On the other hand, as more people experience identity theft, online predation, stalking, awkward photos, etc., support for privacy regulations could grow.

3. There are several examples of self-regulation on the internet. YouTube bans nudity and takes down copyrighted material that is used without permission if informed of the infraction. Computer operating systems routinely are made with parental controls that enable families to filter and monitor their children. Schools also sue filtering systems.

6

THE MASS MEDIA

Sociological Perspectives on the Media
   Functionalist View
   Conflict View
   Feminist View
   Interactionist View

The Audience
   Who Is in the Audience?
   The Segmented Audience
   Audience Behavior

The Media's Global Reach

Social Policy and the Mass Media: Media Concetration
   The Issue

The Setting
Sociological Insights
Policy Initiatives

BOXES

PHOTO ESSAY : *How Does Television Portray the Family*

TAKING SOCIETY TO WORK: *Nicole Martorano Van Cleve, Former Brand Planner, Leo Burnett USA*

RESEARCH TODAY: *The Color of Network TV*

SOCIOLOGY IN THE GLOBAL COMMUNITY: *Al Jazeera is on the Air*

KEY POINTS

Mass Media: By the term **mass media,** sociologists refer to the print and electronic instruments of communication that carry messages to often widespread audiences. The social impact of the mass media in society is obvious. Few aspects of society are as central as the mass media. Through the media, we expand our understanding of people and events beyond what we experience in person. For sociologists, the key questions are how the mass media affect our social institutions and how they influence our social behavior.

The Functionalist View: The most obvious function of the mass media is to entertain. We often think the purpose of the media is to occupy our leisure time, but they also serve other important functions. The media also socialize us, enforce social norms, confer status, and promote consumption. An important dysfunction is that they may act as a narcotic, desensitizing us to events.

Socialization and the Mass Media: The media act as agents of socialization. The media increase social cohesion by presenting a more or less standardized, common view of culture through mass communication. The mass media unquestionably play a significant role in providing a collective experience for members of a society.

Enforcer of Social Norms: The mass media often reaffirm proper behavior by showing what happens to people who act in a way that violates societal expectations.

Conferral of Status and Promotion of Consumption: The mass media confer status on people, organizations, and public issues by singling out one from thousands of other similarly placed issues or people to become significant. Media advertising contributes to a consumer culture that creates "needs" and raises unrealistic expectations of what is required to be happy or satisfied. Moreover, because the media depend heavily on advertising revenue, advertisers are able to influence media content.

Dysfunctional Media—The Narcotizing Effect: Some refer to the media as having a narcotizing dysfunction. A **narcotizing dysfunction** refers to the phenomenon whereby the media provide such massive amounts of information that the audience becomes numb and generally fails to act on the information, regardless of how compelling the issue is.

Conflict View: Conflict theorists emphasize that the media reflect and even exacerbate many of the divisions within our society and world, including those based on gender, race, ethnicity, and social class. Within the mass media, a relatively small number of people control what material eventually reaches the audience, a process known as **gatekeeping**. Conflict theorists argue that the mass media serve to maintain the privileges of certain groups. Moreover, while protecting their own interests, powerful groups may limit the representation of others in the media.

Feminist View: Feminists continue the argument advanced by conflict theorists that the mass media stereotype and misrepresent social reality. They contend that their images of the sexes communicate unrealistic, stereotypical, and limiting perceptions.

Interactionist View: Interactionists are especially interested in shared understandings of everyday behavior. They examine the media on the micro level to see how they shape day-to-day social behavior. The interactionist perspective also helps us to understand more about one important aspect of the entire mass media system—the *audience*.

The Audience: We can look at the audience from the level of both microsociology and macrosociology. At the micro level, we might consider how audience members, interacting among themselves, might respond to the media, or in the case of live performances, actually influence the performers. At the macro level, we might examine broader societal consequences of the media, such as the early childhood education delivered through programming like *Sesame Street*. Despite the role of **opinion leaders** (those who, through day-to-day personal contact and communication, influence the opinions and decisions of others), members of an audience do not all interpret the media in the same way.

The Media Industry: The media industry is getting more and more concentrated, with just a handful of multinational corporations dominating the publishing, broadcasting, and film industries. The one significant exception to centralization and concentration is the Internet.

KEY TERMS

Briefly define or identify the following terms in the spaces provided below. The definitions of these terms can be found later in this chapter of the study guide.

Mass media	Gatekeeping
Narcotizing dysfunction	Dominant ideology

Digital Divide	Opinion leader
Stereotype	

SELF-TEST

MODIFIED TRUE/FALSE QUESTIONS: If the statement below is true, write "true" in the space provided. If the statement is false, briefly correct the error.

1. Sociologists refer to the print and electronic means of communication that carry messages to often widespread audiences as television transmissions.

2. For sociologists, the key questions are how the mass media affect our social institutions and how they influence our social behavior.

3. Television literally serves as a babysitter, or a "playmate," for many children and even infants.

4. While the media can serve to reinforce proper behavior, they don't endorse illicit activities such as drag racing or drug use.

5. In 1997, a federal law required the television networks to provide one free minute for every minute the government bought for a public service announcement with an antidrug message. The networks have fully complied and continue support this law.

6.   Viewer fatigue begins when the viewer experiences eyestrain and sore fingertips from overuse of the remote control.

7.   The mass media constitute a form of big business in which profits are generally more important than the quality of the programming.

8.   In many countries, the government plays a gatekeeping role. A study for the World Bank found that in 97 countries, only five percent of the top five TV stations and only three percent of the largest radio stations are government owned.

9.   The Internet is a means of quick dissemination of information (or misinformation) without going through any significant gatekeeping process.

10.   The Internet is totally without restrictions.

11.   The term media monitoring refers to the monitoring of an individual's media choices and usage without their knowledge.

12.   During the 2007 spring season, prime-time television series more evenly portrayed minorities, demonstrating that the broadcasting industry is no longer supportive of biased programming.

13.   Media observers believe that the networks will need to integrate the ranks of gatekeepers before they achieve true diversity in programming.

14.   American movies make almost all of their profits from American audiences.

15.   There are no exceptions to the centralization and concentration of the media.

MULTIPLE-CHOICE QUESTIONS: Read each question carefully and then select the best answer.

1.   Sociologists consider the mass media to include
        a. newspapers and magazines.
        b. television and radio.
        c. books and the Internet.
        d. all of the above

2.   Which of the following is NOT a form of mass media?
        a. newspapers
        b. films
        c. advertising
        d. none of the above

3.   The most obvious function of the mass media is
        a. to confer status.
        b. to enforce social norms.
        c. to inform us about our social environment.
        d. to entertain.

4.   The mass media increase social cohesion by presenting a more or less standardized, common view of culture through mass communication. This statement reflects which sociological perspective?
    a. the functionalist perspective
    b. the conflict perspective
    c. the interactionist perspective
    d. the dramaturgical perspective

5.   Sociologist Robert Park studied how newspapers helped immigrants to the United States adjust to their environment by changing their customary habits and by teaching them the opinions held by people in their new home country. His study was conducted from which sociological perspective?
    a. the functionalist perspective
    b. the conflict perspective
    c. the interactionist perspective
    d. the dramaturgical perspective

6.   There are problems inherent in the socialization function of the mass media. Many people worry about
    a. the effect of using the television as a "babysitter."
    b. the impact of violent programming on viewer behavior.
    c. the unequal ability of all individuals to purchase televisions.
    d. both a and b

7.   Which of the following was linked to increases in substance use among youths during the 1990s?
    a. a decline in warnings and antidrug messages from the media
    b. proliferation of pro-use messages from the entertainment industry
    c. high levels of tobacco and alcohol product advertising and promotion
    d. all of the above

8.   Regarding media advertising, sociologists are concerned that
    a. it creates unrealistic expectations of what is required to be happy.
    b. it creates new consumer needs.
    c. advertisers are able to influence media content.
    d. all of the above

9. The term narcotizing dysfunction refers to
    a. the role of the mass media in enforcing social norms.
    b. the collection and distribution of information concerning events in the social environment.
    c. the phenomenon whereby the mass media provide such massive amounts of coverage that the audience becomes numb and generally fails to act on the information.
    d. the socialization process.

10. Which sociological perspective is especially concerned with the media's ability to decide what gets transmitted through gatekeeping?
    a. the functionalist perspective
    b. the conflict perspective
    c. the interactionist perspective
    d. the dramaturgical perspective

11. Gatekeeping, the process by which a relatively small number of people control what material reaches an audience, is largely dominant in all but which of the following media?
    a. television
    b. the Internet
    c. publishing
    d. music

12. In the United States, the gatekeeping process is
    a. in the hands of private individuals who desire to maximize profits.
    b. in the hands of political leaders who desire to maintain control of the government.
    c. in the hands of church leaders who desire to maintain control of the government.
    d. none of the above

13. What term is used to describe the set of cultural beliefs and practices that helps to maintain powerful social, economic, and political interests?
    a. conflict ideology
    b. gatekeeping
    c. dominant ideology
    d. cultural ideology

14.   Which of the following is an example of television creating false images or stereotypes of subordinate groups which become accepted as accurate portrayals of reality?
   a.   an all-White cast in an urban-based show situated in an ethnically diverse city
   b.   Blacks being repeatedly portrayed and featured in crime-based dramas
   c.   Latinos rarely being present in any television program
   d.   all of the above

15.   Why should it matter that minority groups aren't visible on network television if they are well represented on cable networks like BET, UPN, and Univision?
   a.   Everyone has the right to be a "star."
   b.   An implication of the equal rights amendment is that all races and nationalities must be equally represented on television.
   c.   A societal backlash may occur because minorities feel slighted by under-representation.
   d.   Whites as well as minorities see a distorted picture of their society every time they turn on network TV.

16.   Which perspective contends that the mass media stereotype and misrepresent social reality, thus influencing the way we view men and women?
   a.   the functionalist perspective
   b.   the conflict perspective
   c.   the interactionist perspective
   d.   the feminist perspective

17.   Which of the following sociological perspectives helps us to understand more about one important aspect of the entire mass media system—the audience?
   a.   the functionalist perspective
   b.   the conflict perspective
   c.   the interactionist perspective
   d.   the feminist perspective

18.   Which perspective examines the media on the micro level to see how they shape day-to-day social behavior?
   a.   the functionalist perspective
   b.   the conflict perspective
   c.   the interactionist perspective
   d.   the feminist perspective

19. Sociologist Paul Lazarfeld and his colleagues pioneered the study of what?
    a. egocasting
    b. narcotizing dysfunction
    c. the media's global reach
    d. media violence

20. In his study of how the social composition of audience members affected how they interpreted news coverage, sociologist Darnell Hunt found what kind of differences in perception?
    a. racial
    b. gender
    c. class
    d. religious

21. Which of the following is the key to creating a truly global network that reaches directly into workplaces, schools, and homes?
    a. cable networks
    b. XFM radio broadcasting
    c. distribution of major print media
    d. the Internet

22. Sociologist Todd Gitlin uses the term _____ to describe the way in which the media permeates all aspects of everyday life.
    a. global reach
    b. global village
    c. global torrent
    d. globalization

23. Which of the following statements about the televised news network Al Jazeera is true?
    a. Everyone agrees that Al Jazeera is far more biased than CNN or ABC.
    b. Since September 11, 2001, Al Jazeera has steadfastly refused to air videotaped messages from Osama bin Laden.
    c. Al Jazeera presents a diversity of viewpoints.
    d. Almost all of the Arab world would agree that Palestinian suicide bombings are wrong.

24.   What is the tem for the relative lack of access to the latest technologies among low-income groups, racial and ethnic minorities, rural residents, and the citizens of developing countries?
    a. the technology gap
    b. media concentration
    c. the digital divide
    d. the digital gap

25.   According to the most recent FCC data, what percentage of television stations are owned by members of racial or ethnic minority groups?
    a. 4 percent
    b. 8 percent
    c. 10 percent
    d. 12 percent

FILL-IN QUESTIONS: Fill in the blank spaces in the sentences below with the correct words. Where two or more words are required, there will be a corresponding number of blank spaces.

1.   For sociologists, the key question is how the mass media affect our _____ _____ and how they influence our _____ _____.

2.   In 1997, a federal law required television networks to provide one free minute for every minute the government bought for a public service announcement with a(n) _____ message.

3.   Paul Lazarsfeld and Robert Merton created the term _____ _____ to refer to the phenomenon whereby the media provide such massive amounts of information that the audience becomes numb and generally fails to act on the information, regardless of how compelling the issue.

4.   The content of the media may create false images or _____ of subordinate groups.

5.   The fact that, in 2006, the U.S. government tried to obtain records of Americans' web-browsing activities points to concerns about _____ _____.

6.   The _____ perspective contends that television distorts the political process.

7.   We risk being _____ if we overstress U.S. dominance and assume that other nations do not play a role in media cultural exports.

8.   Efforts by _____ to monitor media content that crosses the borders of developing nations was one factor that prompted the United States to withdraw from this U.N. organization in the mid-1980s.

9.   The fact that pornography presents women as sex objects is one reason why it is a troubling and continuing issue for _____.

10.   _____ examine the media on the micro level to see how they shape day-to-day social behavior.

11.   The _____ perspective helps us to understand more about one important aspect of the entire mass media system, the _____.

12.   We can point to a handful of _____ _____ that dominate the publishing, broadcasting, and film industries.

13.   Today, _____ _____ is no longer a barrier, and instant messaging is possible across the world.

14.   According to the _____ theory, global trade in the media facilitates the exchange of intellectual property.

15.   By 2007, Internet advertising revenue is expected to _____ total television ad revenue.

UNDERSTANDING SOCIAL POLICY: Each of the following questions is based on material that appears in the social policy section on "Media Concentration." Write a brief answer to each question in the space provided below.

1.   How do the sociological perspectives view media concentration?

2.   Why can the Internet said to be an exception to media concentration?

3.   How has big business responded to the Internet?

DEFINITIONS OF KEY TERMS

Mass media: Print and electronic means of communication that carry messages to widespread audiences.

Narcotizing dysfunction: The phenomenon in which the media provide such massive amounts of coverage that the audience becomes numb and fails to act on the information, regardless of how compelling the issue.

Gatekeeping: The process by which a relatively small number of people in the media industry control what material eventually reaches the audience.

Dominant ideology: A set of cultural beliefs and practices that helps to maintain powerful social, economic, and political interests.

Digital divide: The relative lack of access to the latest technologies among low-income groups, racial and ethnic minorities, rural residents, and the citizens of developing countries.

Stereotype: An unreliable generalization about all members of a group that does not recognize individual differences within the group.

Opinion leader: Someone who influences the opinions and decisions of others through day-to-day personal contact and communication.

ANSWERS TO SELF-TEST

Modified True/False Questions

1.   Sociologists refer to the print and electronic means of communication that carry messages to often widespread audiences as the mass media.

2.   True

3.   True

4.   While the media can serve to reinforce proper behavior, they may also endorse illicit activity, such as physical violence or drug abuse.

5.   In 1997, a federal law required the television networks to provide one free minute for every minute the government bought for a public service announcement with an antidrug message. However, the networks subsequently made an agreement with the government to drop the free minutes in exchange for embedding aggressive antidrug messages in their programs (e.g., *ER* and *The Practice*).

6. Viewer fatigue sets in sometime after a tragedy, such as a natural disaster or family crisis.

7. True

8. The study for the World Bank found that in 97 countries, 60 percent of the top five TV stations and 72 percent of the largest radio stations are government owned.

9. True

10. The Internet is not totally without restrictions. Laws in many nations try to regulate content on such issues as gambling, pornography, and even political views; and popular Internet service providers will terminate accounts for offensive behavior.

11. True

12. During the 2007 season, only 5 of the primetime series featured performers of color in leading roles.

13. True

14. Many motion pictures, such as *The Titanic*, have brought in more revenues abroad than at home.

15. There is one exception to the centralization and concentration of the media—the Internet.

Multiple-Choice Questions

1.	d	10.	b	19.	b
2.	d	11.	b	20.	a
3.	d	12.	a	21.	d
4.	a	13.	c	22.	c
5.	a	14.	d	23.	c
6.	d	15.	d	24.	c
7.	b	16.	d	25.	b
8.	d	17.	c		
9.	c	18.	c		

Fill-In Questions

1. social institutions; social behavior
2. antidrug
3. narcotizing dysfunction
4. stereotypes
5. media monitoring
6. conflict
7. ethnocentric
8. UNESCO
9. feminists
10. Interactionists
11. interactionist; audience
12. multinational corporations
13. physical distance
14. functionalist
15. surpass

Understanding Social Policy: Media Concentration

1. Functionalists emphasize that consolidation in any industry leads to greater economic efficiency. Conflict theorists believe that concentration stifles opportunity for minority ownership and representation in the media in the U.S. and worldwide. Interactionists are interested in the ways in which the Internet has changed how people get news and using the Internet in place of face-to-face communication.

2. The Internet is an exception because anyone with access to a computer may access sites, email, etc. People can exchange media, create their own media content, post it, and distribute it.

3. Big business has successfully lobbied for continued deregulation, which allows increasing concentration of ownership. Big business see the growth of the Internet as a new source of revenue and hope to profit from it.

NOTES

CHAPTER

7 DEVIANCE AND SOCIAL CONTROL

Social Control

    Conformity and Obedience

    Informal and Formal Social Control

    Law and Society

What is Deviance?

    Deviance and the Social Stigma

    Deviance and Technology

Sociological Perspectives on Deviance

    Functionalist Perspective

    Interactionist Perspective

    Labeling Theory

    Conflict Theory

    Feminist Perspective

Crime

    Types of Crime

    Crime Statistics

Social Policy and Social Control: The Death Penalty in the United States and Worldwide

    The Issue

    The Setting

    Sociological Insights

    Policy Initiatives

BOXES

    SOCIOLOGY ON CAMPUS: Binge Drinking

    SOCIOLOGY ON CAMPUS: Campus Crime

    RESEARCH IN TODAY: The Social Construction of Crime: Road Rage

    TAKING SOCIOLOGY TO WORK: Stephanie Vezzani, Special Agent, U.S. Secret Service

| **KEY POINTS**

Social Control: The term **social control** refers to the techniques and strategies for preventing deviant human behavior in any society. Social control occurs on all levels of society: in the family, in peer groups, and in bureaucratic organizations. Most of us respect and accept basic social norms and assume that others will do the same. If we fail to live up to a norm, we may face punishment through informal **sanctions,** such as fear and ridicule, or formal sanctions, such as jail sentences or fines.

Conformity and Obedience: Stanley Milgram made a useful distinction between two important levels of social control. He used the term **conformity** to mean going along with one's peers—individuals of our own status who have no special right to direct our behavior. In contrast, **obedience** is compliance with higher authorities in a hierarchical structure.

Informal and Formal Social Control: **Informal social control** is social control carried out by people casually through such means as smiles, laughter, and ridicule. **Formal social control** is carried out by authorized agents, such as police officers, school administrators, employers, military officers, and managers of movie theaters. It can serve as a last resort when socialization and informal sanctions do not bring about desired behavior.

Law and Society: Some norms are so important to a society that they are formalized into laws controlling people's behavior. **Law** is governmental social control. Sociologists see the creation of laws as a social process. In their view, law is not merely a static body of rules handed down from generation to generation; rather, it reflects continually changing standards of what is right and wrong, of how violations are to be determined, and of what sanctions are to be applied.

Deviance: For sociologists, **deviance** is behavior that violates the standards of conduct or expectations of a group or society. Deviance involves the violations of group norms, which may or may not be formalized into law. It is a comprehensive concept that includes not only criminal behavior but also many actions that are not subject to prosecution. Deviance can be understood only within its social context.

Deviance and Social Stigma: While deviance can include relatively minor day-to-day decisions about our personal behavior, in some cases it can become part of a person's identity. This process is called stigmatization. The interactionist Erving Goffman coined the term **stigma** to describe the labels society uses to devalue members of certain social groups. Often people are stigmatized for deviant behaviors they may no longer engage in. Goffman draws a useful distinction between a prestige symbol that draws attention to a positive aspect of one's identity, such as a wedding band or a badge, and a stigma symbol that discredits or debases one's identity, such as a conviction for child molestation.

The Functionalist View: According to functionalists, deviance is a common part of human existence, with positive (as well as negative) consequences for social stability. Deviance helps to define the limits of proper behavior. As Émile Durkheim observed, the punishments established within a culture (including both formal and informal mechanisms of social control) help to define acceptable behavior and thus contribute to stability. If improper acts were not sanctioned, people might stretch their standards as to what constitutes appropriate conduct.

Merton's Theory of Deviance: Using a functionalist analysis, Robert Merton adapted Durkheim's notion of anomie to explain why people accept or reject the goals of a society, the socially approved means of fulfilling their aspirations, or both. Merton developed the **anomie theory of deviance**, which posits five basic forms of adaptation. (1) Conformity to social norms, the most common adaptation in Merton's typology, is the opposite of deviance. It involves acceptance of both the overall societal goal and the approved means. (2) The "innovator" accepts the goals of society but pursues them with means that are regarded as improper. (3) The "ritualist" has abandoned the goal of material success and becomes compulsively committed to the institutional means. (4) The "retreatist" has withdrawn from both the goals and the means of a society, and (5) the "rebel" feels alienated from the dominant means and goals, and may seek a dramatically different social order.

Cultural Transmission and Differential Association: Sociologist Edwin Sutherland drew upon the **cultural transmission** school of criminology, which emphasizes that criminal behavior is learned through interactions with others. Sutherland maintained that through interactions with a primary group and significant others, people acquire definitions of proper and improper behavior. He used the term **differential association** to describe the process through which exposure to attitudes favorable to criminal acts leads to the violation of rules. People are more likely to engage in norm-defying behavior if they are part of a group or subculture that stresses deviant values.

Labeling Theory: Reflecting the contribution of interactionist theorists, labeling theory attempts to explain why certain people are perceived as deviants, while others with similar behavior are not. Labeling theory is also called the **societal-reaction approach**, reminding us that it is the response to an act, not the behavior itself, which determines deviance. An important aspect of labeling theory is the recognition that some people or groups have the power to define labels and apply them to others. The popularity of labeling theory is reflected in the emergence of a related perspective called social constructionism. According to the **social constructionist perspective**, deviance is the product of the culture we live in. Social constructionists focus specifically on the decision-making process that creates the deviant identity.

Conflict View of Deviance: Sociologist Richard Quinney and other conflict theorists argue that lawmaking is often an attempt by the powerful to coerce others into their own brand of morality. Crime, according to Quinney, is a definition of conduct created by authorized agents of social control in a politically organized society. This theory helps to explain why gambling and drug usage are illegal.

Feminist Perspective: When it comes to crime and to deviance in general, society tends to treat women in a stereotypical fashion. Cultural views and attitudes toward women influence how they are perceived and labeled. The feminist perspective also emphasizes that deviance, including crime, tends to flow from economic relationships.

Crime Statistics: Crime statistics are not as accurate as social scientists would like. Reported crime is very high in the United States, and the public regards crime as a major social problem. However, there has been a significant decline in violent crime nationwide following many years of increases. Sociologists have several ways of measuring crime. Partly because of the deficiencies in official statistics, the National Crime Victimization Survey was initiated in 1972. The Bureau of Justice Statistics, in compiling this annual report, seeks information from law enforcement agencies, but also interviews members of over 84,000 households and asks if they have been victims of a specific set of crimes. In general, **victimization surveys** question ordinary people, not police officers, to learn how much crime occurs.

International Crime Rates: During the 1980s and 1990s, violent crimes were much more common in the United States than in Western Europe. Yet, the incidence of certain other types of crime appears to be higher elsewhere. For example, England, Italy, Australia, and New Zealand all have higher rates of car theft than the United States does.

KEY TERMS

Briefly define or identify the following terms in the spaces provided below. The definitions of these terms can be found later in this chapter of the study guide.

Social control	Obedience
Sanction	Informal social control
Conformity	Formal social control

Law	Social constructionist perspective
Control theory	Differential justice
Deviance	Crime
Stigma	Index crimes
Anomie	Victimless crime
Anomie theory of deviance	Professional criminal
Cultural transmission	Organized crime
Differential association	White-collar crime
Routine activities theory	Transnational crime
Labeling theory	Victimization survey
Societal reaction approach	Social disorganization theory

SELF-TEST

MODIFIED TRUE/FALSE QUESTIONS: If the statement below is true, write "true" in the space provided. If the statement is false, briefly correct the error.

1. A recruit entering military service will typically obey the habits and language of other recruits, and will conform to the orders of superior officers.

2. Viewed from an interactionist perspective, one important aspect of Milgram's findings concerning obedience to authority is that subjects in follow-up studies were more likely to inflict the supposed shocks as they were moved physically closer to their victims.

3. A 1998 policy statement by the American Academy of Pediatrics that corporal punishment is not effective, and can indeed be harmful, is supported by the majority of child development specialists and pediatricians in the United States.

4. In the view of sociologists, law is a static body of rules handed down from generation to generation.

5. Binge drinking is always regarded as deviant behavior.

6. Conflict theory suggests that our connection to members of society leads us to systematically conform to society's norms.

7. According to functionalists, deviance has only negative consequences for social stability.

8.   Robert Merton made a key contribution to sociological understanding of deviance by pointing out that deviants such as innovators and ritualists share a great deal with conforming people.

9.   Sociologist Edwin Sutherland popularized labeling theory.

10.   Researchers have found that discretionary differences in the way social control is exercised puts deprived African Americans and Hispanics at a disadvantage in the justice system—both as juveniles and as adults.

11.   Organized crime dominates the world of illegal business, just as large corporations dominate the conventional business world.

12.   Conviction for a white-collar crime has serious implications for an individual's reputation and career aspirations.

13.   The conflict perspective argues that the criminal justice system largely disregards the white-collar crimes of the affluent, while focusing on crimes committed by the poor.

14.   Trafficking in human beings, sea piracy, and terrorism are among the most common types of transnational crime.

15.   Sociologists agree that the high rates of violent crimes in the United States are the result of the emphasis our society places on individual economic achievement.

MULTIPLE-CHOICE QUESTIONS: Read each question carefully and then select the best answer.

1.   If we fail to respect and obey social norms, we may face punishment through informal or formal
   a. techniques of neutralization.
   b. deviance.
   c. cultural transmission.
   d. sanctions.

2.   Which sociological perspective emphasizes that societies literally could not function if massive numbers of people defied standards of appropriate conduct?
   a. the functionalist perspective
   b. the conflict perspective
   c. the interactionist perspective
   d. labeling theory

3.   A useful distinction between conformity and obedience was made by social psychologist
   a. Richard Quinney.
   b. Émile Durkheim.
   c. Edwin Sutherland.
   d. Stanley Milgram.

4.   Milgram used the term conformity to mean
   a. going along with peers.
   b. compliance with higher authorities in a hierarchical structure.
   c. the techniques and strategies for preventing deviant human behavior in any society.
   d. penalties and rewards for conduct concerning a norm.

5.   Which of the following is NOT an example of informal social control?
   a.   jail
   b.   laughter
   c.   raising an eyebrow
   d.   ridicule

6.   Your text tells us that almost one out of every _____ adult Americans undergoes some form of correctional supervision—jail, prison, probation, or parole—every year.
   a.   30
   b.   40
   c.   50
   d.   60

7.   Which sociological theory suggests that our connection to members of society leads us to conform systematically to society's norms?
   a.   feminist theory
   b.   control theory
   c.   interactionist theory
   d.   functionalist theory

8.   Deviance is
   a.   always criminal behavior.
   b.   behavior that violates the standards of conduct or expectations of a group or society.
   c.   perverse behavior.
   d.   inappropriate behavior that cuts across all cultures and social orders.

9.   Which sociologist coined the term "stigma" to describe the labels society uses to devalue members of certain social groups?
   a.   Charles Horton Cooley
   b.   George Herbert Mead
   c.   Émile Durkheim
   d.   Erving Goffman

10. Which of the following suggested that the punishments established within a culture help to define acceptable behavior, and thus contribute to stability?
    a. William Chambliss
    b. Émile Durkheim
    c. Richard Quinney
    d. Stanley Milgram

11. In Robert Merton's anomie theory of deviance, the most common adaptation is
    a. conformity.
    b. innovation.
    c. ritualism.
    d. rebellion.

12. A burglar who wants to live in the suburbs along with lawyers and stockbrokers will pursue material success by violating the law. In Merton's terms, the burglar is a(n)
    a. ritualist.
    b. retreatist.
    c. rebel.
    d. innovator.

13. In Merton's terms, a bureaucratic official who blindly applies rules and regulations without remembering the larger goals of the organization would be a(n)
    a. ritualist.
    b. retreatist.
    c. rebel.
    d. innovator.

14. Which theory contends that criminal victimization increases when motivated offenders and suitable targets converge?
    a. differential association theory
    b. labeling theory
    c. conflict theory
    d. routine activities theory

15. Which of the following conducted observation research on two groups of high school males (the Saints and the Roughnecks) and concluded that social class played an important role in the varying fortunes of the two groups?
    a. Richard Quinney
    b. Edwin Sutherland
    c. Émile Durkheim
    d. William Chambliss

16. Howard Becker is associated with which approach to deviance?
    a. labeling
    b. anomie
    c. routine activities
    d. differential association

17. Labeling theory is also called the _____ approach.
    a. conflict
    b. functionalist
    c. societal-reaction
    d. stigmatization

18. An important aspect of labeling theory is the recognition that some people or groups have the power to define labels and apply them to others. This view recalls the emphasis placed on the social significance of power by the
    a. functionalist perspective.
    b. conflict perspective.
    c. interactionist perspective.
    d. anomie theory of deviance.

19. Which of the following is a leading exponent of the view that the criminal justice system serves the interests of the powerful?
    a. Richard Quinney
    b. Edwin Sutherland
    c. Stanley Milgram
    d. William Chambliss

20. _____ view standards of deviant behavior as merely reflecting cultural norms, whereas _____ and _____ theorists point out that the most powerful groups in a society can shape laws and standards and determine who is (or is not) prosecuted as a criminal.
    a. Conflict theorists; functionalists; labeling
    b. Labeling theorists; functionalists; conflict
    c. Functionalists; conflict; labeling
    d. Conflict theorists; interactionists; labeling;

21. Gambling, prostitution, and smoking marijuana are
    a. white-collar crimes.
    b. violent crimes.
    c. victimless crimes.
    d. organized crime.

22. Which of the following offered pioneering insights regarding professional criminals by publishing an annotated account written by a professional thief?
    a. Robert Merton
    b. Émile Durkheim
    c. Howard S. Becker
    d. Edwin Sutherland

23. Which of the following terms did sociologist Daniel Bell use to describe the sequential passage of organized crime leadership from Irish Americans in the early part of the twentieth century to Jewish Americans in the 1920s and then to Italian Americans in the early 1930s?
    a. ethnic succession
    b. victimless crime
    c. differential association
    d. routine activity approach

24. Which of the following is considered a white-collar crime?
    a. consumer fraud
    b. bribery
    c. income-tax evasion
    d. all of the above

25. Crime rates for which of the following crimes was higher in the United States than in Europe during the 1980s and 1990s?
    a. murder
    b. rape
    c. robbery
    d. all of the above

FILL-IN QUESTIONS: Fill in the blank spaces in the sentences below with the correct words. Where two or more words are required, there will be a corresponding number of blank spaces.

1. _____ theorists are concerned that "successful functioning" of a society will consistently benefit the powerful and work to the disadvantage of other groups.

2. In the United States, one common and controversial example of _____ social control is parental use of corporal punishment.

3. _____ social control is carried out by authorized agents, such as police officers, judges, administrators, employers, military officers, and managers of movie theaters.

4. Some norms are considered so important by a society that they are formalized into _____ controlling people's behavior.

5. It is important to underscore the fact that _____ is the primary source of conformity and obedience, including obedience to law.

6. _____ involves the violation of group norms that may or may not be formalized into law.

7. In general, sociologists reject any emphasis on _____ roots of crime and deviance.

8. _____ is a state of normlessness that typically occurs during a period of profound social change and disorder, such as a time of economic collapse.

9.   Sociologist _____ _____ advanced the argument than an individual undergoes the same basic socialization process whether learning conforming or deviant acts.

10.   _____ _____ _____, a recent interactionist explanation of deviance, considers that for the requisite conditions for a crime or deviant act to occur, there must be at the same time and in the same place a perpetrator, a victim, and/or an object of property.

11.   _____ theorists argue that lawmaking is often an attempt by the powerful to coerce others into their own brand of morality.

12.   _____ represents some type of deviation from formal social norms administered by the state.

13.   Organizations such as Mothers Against Drunk Driving (MADD) and Students Against Drunk Driving (SADD) have had success in recent years in shifting public attitudes regarding drunkenness, so that it is no longer viewed as a "_____ crime."

14.   Daniel Bell used the term _____ _____ to describe the process during which leadership of organized crime was transferred from Irish Americans to Jewish Americans and later to Italian Americans and others.

15.   The most serious limitation of official crime statistics is that they include only those crimes actually _____ to law enforcement agencies.

UNDERSTANDING SOCIAL POLICY: Each of the following questions is based on material that appears in the social policy section on "The Death Penalty." Write a brief answer to each question in the space provided below.

1.   How common is the death penalty, both worldwide and in the United States?

2.   What is the functionalist view of the death penalty?

3.   What is the conflict view of the death penalty?

DEFINITIONS OF KEY TERMS

Social control: The techniques and strategies for preventing deviant human behavior in any society.

Sanction: A penalty or reward for conduct concerning a social norm.

Conformity: Going along with one's peers—individuals of our own status, who have no special right to direct our behavior.

Obedience: Compliance with higher authorities in a hierarchical structure.

Informal social control: Social control that is carried out casually by ordinary people through such means as laughter, smiles, and ridicule.

Formal social control: Social control that is carried out by authorized agents, such as police officers, judges, school administrators, and employers.

Law: Governmental social control.

Control theory: A view of conformity and deviance that suggests that our connection to members of society leads us to systematically conform to society's norms.

Deviance: Behavior that violates the standards of conduct or expectations of a group or society.

Stigma: A label used to devalue members of certain social groups.

Social disorganization theory: An approach to deviance that attributes increase in crime and deviance to the absence or breakdown of communal relationships and social institutions.

Anomie: Durkheim's term for the loss of direction felt in a society when social control of individual behavior has become ineffective.

Anomie theory of deviance: Robert Merton's theory of deviance as an adaptation of socially prescribed goals or of the means governing their attainment, or both.

Cultural transmission: A school of criminology that argues that criminal behavior is learned through social interactions.

Differential association: A theory of deviance proposed by Edwin Sutherland that holds that violation of rules results from exposure to attitudes favorable to criminal acts.

Routine activities theory: The notion that criminal victimization increases when motivated offenders and suitable targets converge.

Labeling theory: An approach to deviance that attempts to explain why certain people are viewed as deviants while others engaged in the same behavior are not.

Societal-reaction approach: Another name for *labeling theory*.

Social constructionist perspective: An approach to deviance that emphasizes the role of culture in the creation of the deviant identity.

Differential justice: Differences in the way social control is exercised over different groups.

Crime: A violation of criminal law for which some governmental authority applies formal penalties.

Index crimes: The eight types of crime reported annually by the FBI in the Uniform Crime Reports: murder, rape, robbery, assault, burglary, theft, motor vehicle theft, and arson.

Victimless crime: A term used by sociologists to describe the willing exchange among adults of widely desired, but illegal, goods and services.

Professional criminal: A person who pursues crime as a day-to-day occupation, developing skilled techniques and enjoying a certain degree of status among other criminals.

Organized crime: The work of a group that regulates relations among criminal enterprises involved in illegal activities, including prostitution, gambling, and the smuggling and sale of drugs.

White-collar crime: Illegal acts committed by affluent, "respectable" individuals in the course of business activities.

Transnational crime: Crime that occurs across multiple national borders.

Victimization survey: A questionnaire or interview given to a sample of the population to determine whether people have been victims of crime.

ANSWERS TO SELF-TEST

Modified True/False Questions

1. A recruit entering military service will typically *conform* to the habits and language of other recruits, and will obey the orders of superior officers.

2. Viewed from an interactionist perspective, one important aspect of Milgram's findings is that subjects in follow-up studies were *less* likely to inflict the supposed shocks as they were moved physically closer to their victims.

3. Despite a 1998 policy statement by the American Academy of Pediatrics that corporal punishment is not effective and can be harmful, 59 percent of pediatricians support the use of corporal punishment.

4. In the view of sociologists, law is not merely a static body of rules handed down from generation to generation. Rather, it reflects continually changing standards of what is right and wrong, of how violations are to be determined, and of what sanctions are to be applied.

5. On the one hand, binge drinking can be regarded as deviant, violating the standards of conduct expected of those in an academic setting. The other side of this potentially self-destructive behavior is that binge drinking represents conformity to the peer culture.

6. Control theory suggests that our connection to members of society leads us to systematically conform to society's norms.

7. According to functionalists, deviance is a normal part of human existence, with positive (as well as negative) consequences for social stability.

8. True

9. Sociologist Howard S. Becker popularized labeling theory.

10. True

11. True

12. Conviction for white-collar crimes does not generally harm a person's reputation and career aspirations nearly as much as conviction for a street crime would.

13. True

14. True

15. Sociologists suggest that the United States places a greater emphasis on individual economic achievement than do other societies; tolerates, if not condones, many forms of violence; has sharp disparities between poor and affluent citizens; has significant unemployment; and has substantial alcohol and drug abuse. These factors combine to produce a climate conducive to crime.

Multiple-Choice Questions

1.	d	10.	b	19.	a
2.	a	11.	a	20.	c
3.	d	12.	d	21.	c
4.	a	13.	a	22.	d
5.	a	14.	d	23.	a
6.	a	15.	d	24.	d
7.	b	16.	a	25.	d
8.	b	17.	c		
9.	d	18.	b		

Fill-In Questions

1.	Conflict	9.	Edwin Sutherland
2.	informal	10.	Routine activities theory
3.	Formal	11.	Conflict
4.	laws	12.	Crime
5.	socialization	13.	victimless
6.	Deviance	14.	ethnic succession
7.	genetic	15.	reported
8.	Anomie		

Understanding Social Policy: The Death Penalty

1.   Worldwide, less than half of all nations allow the death penalty. At least 3,797 prisoners in 25 countries are known to have been executed in 2004 alone, and another 7,395 defendants in 64 nations were sentenced to death that year. Ninety-seven percent of all known executions in 2004 took place in China, Iran, Viet Nam, and the United States. Within the United States, 38 states, the military, and the federal government continue to sentence convicted felons to death for selected crimes. On the state level, more than 1,010 prisoners have been executed since 1977.

2.   Viewed from the functionalist perspective of Émile Durkheim, sanctions against deviant acts help to reinforce society's standards of proper behavior. In this light, supporters of capital punishment insist that fear of execution will prevent at least some criminals from committing serious offenses. While proponents note the functions of the death penalty, there are some dysfunctions. Though many citizens are concerned that the alternative to execution, life in prison, is unnecessarily expensive, sentencing a person to death is not cheap.

3.   The conflict perspective emphasizes the persistence of social inequality in today's society. Simply put, poor people cannot afford to hire the best lawyers, but must rely on court-appointed attorneys who typically are overworked and underpaid. Another issue of concern to conflict theorists and researchers is the possibility of racial discrimination.

STRATIFICATION AND SOCIAL MOBILITY IN THE UNITED STATES

Systems of Stratification

   Slavery

   Castes

   Estates

   Social Classes

Perspectives on Stratification

   Karl Marx's View of Class Differences

   Max Weber's View of Stratification

   Interactionist View

Is Stratification Universal?

   Functionalist View

   Conflict View

   Lenski's View

Stratification by Social Class

   Measuring Social Class

   Wealth and Income

   Poverty

   Life Chances

Social Mobility

   Open versus Closed Stratification Systems

   Types of Social Mobility

Social Mobility in the United States

Social Policy and Stratification: Rethinking Welfare in North America and Europe

   The Issue

   The Setting

   Sociological Insights

   Policy Initiatives

BOXES

   TAKING SOCIOLOGY TO WORK: *Jessica Houston Su, Research Assistant, Joblessness and Urban Poverty Research Program*

   RESEARCH TODAY: *The Shrinking Middle Class*

   SOCIOLOGY IN THE GLOBAL COMMUNITY: *It's All Relative--- Appalachian Poverty and Congolese Affluence*

   SOCIOLOGY ON CAMPUS: *Social Class and Financial Aid*

| KEY POINTS

Stratification and Social Inequality: The term **social inequality** describes a condition in which members of society have different amounts of wealth, prestige, or power. Some degree of social inequality characterizes every society. When a system of social inequality is based on a hierarchy of groups, sociologists refer to it as **stratification**: a structured ranking of entire groups of people that perpetuates unequal economic rewards and power in a society. **Ascribed status** is a social position "assigned" to a person without regard for that person's unique characteristics or talents. By contrast, **achieved status** is a social position attained by a person largely through his or her own efforts.

The Class System of the United States: Sociologist Daniel Rossides has conceptualized the class system of the United States using a five-class model. Rossides categorizes about 1 to 2 percent of the people in the United States as upper class. In contrast, the lower class, which is approximately 20 to 25 percent of the population, disproportionately consists of Blacks, Hispanics, single mothers with dependent children, and people who cannot find regular work or must make do with low-paying jobs. Sandwiched between the upper and lower classes in Rossides's model are the upper-middle class, the lower-middle class, and the working class.

Karl Marx's View of Class Differentiation: Karl Marx viewed class differentiation as the crucial determinant of social, economic, and political inequality. Marx focused on the two classes that began to emerge as the estate system declined: the bourgeoisie and the proletariat. The **bourgeoisie**, or capitalist class, owns the means of production, such as factories and machinery, while the **proletariat** is the working class. According to Marx, exploitation of the proletariat will inevitably lead to the destruction of the capitalist system. Ultimately, the proletariat will overthrow the rule of the bourgeoisie and the government (which Marx saw as representing the interests of capitalists).

Max Weber's View of Stratification: Unlike Karl Marx, Max Weber insisted that no single characteristic (such as class) totally defines a person's position within the stratification system. He identified three distinct components of stratification: class, status, and power. A person's position in a stratification system reflects some combination of his or her class, status, and power.

The Functionalist View of Stratification: In the view of Kingsley Davis and Wilbert Moore, society must distribute its members among a variety of social positions. Davis and Moore argue that stratification is universal and that social inequality is necessary so that people will be motivated to fill functionally important positions. However, critics note that even if stratification is inevitable, the functionalist explanation for differential rewards does not explain the wide disparity between the rich and the poor.

The Conflict View of Stratification: Contemporary conflict theorists believe that human beings are prone to conflict over scarce resources such as wealth, status, and power. However, Marx focused primarily on class conflict. More recent theorists have extended the analysis to include conflicts based on gender, race, age, and other dimensions. Conflict theorists see stratification as a major source of societal tension and conflict. They do not agree that stratification is functional for a society or that it serves as a source of stability. Rather, conflict sociologists argue that stratification will inevitably lead to instability and to social change.

Lenski's View of Stratification: Gerhard Lenski described how economic systems change as their level of technology becomes more complex, beginning with hunting and gathering and culminating eventually with industrial society. As a society advances in technology, it becomes capable of producing a considerable surplus of goods. The emergence of surplus resources greatly expands the possibilities for inequality in status, influence, and power, and allows a well-defined, rigid class system to develop.

Wealth and Income in the United States: By all measures, income in the United States is unevenly distributed. In 2004, members of the richest fifth (or top 20 percent) of the nation's population earned $88,029 or more. Wealth in the United States is much less evenly distributed than income is. In 2001, the richest fifth of the population held 84.5 percent of the nation's wealth.

Poverty in the United States: Approximately one out of every nine people in this country lives below the poverty line established by the federal government. In 2004, 51 percent of poor people in the United States were living in central cities. According to many observers, the plight of the urban poor is growing worse because of the devastating interplay of inadequate education and limited employment prospects. William Julius Wilson and other social scientists have used the term **underclass** to describe long-term poor people who lack training and skills.

Social Mobility in the United States: The belief in upward social mobility is an important value in our society. Occupational mobility (which can be intergenerational or intragenerational) has been common among males. The impact of education on mobility has diminished somewhat in the last decade. However, occupational mobility among African Americans remains sharply limited by racial discrimination. Gender, like race, is an important factor in one's mobility. In contrast to men, women have a rather large range of clerical occupations open to them. But the modest salary ranges and the few prospects for advancement in many of these positions mean that there is not much possibility of upward mobility.

Rethinking Welfare in North America and Europe: In 1996, the Personal Responsibility and Work Opportunity Reconciliation Act ended the long-standing federal guarantee of assistance to every poor family that meets eligibility requirements. The law set a lifetime limit of five years of welfare benefits, and required all able-bodied adults to work after receiving two years of benefits (although hardship exceptions were allowed). From a conflict perspective, this backlash against welfare recipients reflects deep fears and hostility toward the nation's urban, predominantly African American and Hispanic underclass. Those who take a conflict perspective also urge policy makers and the general public to look closely at **corporate welfare**, the tax breaks, direct payments, and grants that the government makes to corporations—rather than focus on the relatively small allowances being given to welfare mothers and their children.

KEY TERMS

Briefly define or identify the following terms in the spaces provided below. The definitions of these terms can be found later in this chapter of the study guide.

Social inequality	Estate system
Stratification	Class system
Income	Capitalism
Wealth	Bourgeoisie
Ascribed status	Proletariat
Achieved status	Class consciousness
Slavery	False consciousness
Caste	Class

Status group	Life chances
Digital divide	Social mobility
Power	Open system
Dominant ideology	Closed system
Objective method	Horizontal mobility
Prestige	Vertical mobility
Esteem	Intergenerational mobility
Absolute poverty	Intragenerational mobility
Relative poverty	Corporate welfare
Underclass	Socioeconomic status (SES)

SELF-TEST

MODIFIED TRUE/FALSE QUESTIONS: If the statement below is true, write "true" in the space provided. If the statement is false, briefly correct the error.

1.   In ancient Greece, slave status was permanent.

2.   Although the UN Declaration of Human Rights prohibits slavery in all its forms, millions of people around the world still live as slaves.

3.   In recent decades, political reforms have led to the end of India's famous caste system.

4.   According to Daniel Rossides, the largest social class in the United States is the upper-middle class.

5.   Unlike Karl Marx, Max Weber insisted that no single characteristic (such as class) totally defines a person's position within the stratification system.

6.   Max Weber suggested that a person's status cannot diverge from his or her economic class standing.

7.   Social science research has found that inequality exists in all societies—even the simplest.

8.   Conflict sociologists argue that stratification will inevitably lead to instability and to social change.

9.   The objective method of measuring social class views class largely as a social category rather than as a statistical one.

10. For many years, studies of social class tended to neglect the occupations and incomes of women as determinants of social rank.

11. Because federal tax policies of the past three decades have favored low-income Americans, the gap in income between rich Americans and others is now smaller than before.

12. A key factor in the feminization of poverty has been the increase in families with women as single heads of households.

13. Herbert Gans notes that the presence of poor people means that society's dirty work—physically dirty or dangerous, dead-end and underpaid, undignified and menial jobs—will be performed at low cost.

14. One trend in student financial aid is that colleges and universities are increasing the proportion of funds allocated as grants.

15. Gender has little influence in shaping social mobility within the United States.

MULTIPLE-CHOICE QUESTIONS: Read each question carefully and then select the best answer.

1. The term _____ describes a condition in which members of a society have different amounts of wealth, prestige, or power.
   a. stratification
   b. status inconsistency
   c. slavery
   d. social inequality

2. Which of the following is NOT an example of income?
    a. salaries
    b. property
    c. wages
    d. All of the above are examples of income.

3. The most extreme form of legalized social inequality for individuals or groups is
    a. slavery.
    b. open class systems.
    c. closed caste systems.
    d. caste systems.

4. The caste system is generally associated with
    a. Hinduism.
    b. Islam.
    c. Judaism.
    d. Buddhism.

5. In sociologist Daniel Rossides's model of the class system of the United States, the class with the smallest proportion of the population is the
    a. upper class.
    b. upper-middle class.
    c. lower-middle class.
    d. lower class.

6. Compared to the 1960s, the proportion of Americans considered to be middle class today is
    a. declining.
    b. growing.
    c. growing dramatically.
    d. about the same.

7. In Karl Marx's view, the destruction of the capitalist system will occur only if the working class first develops _____ consciousness.
    a. bourgeois
    b. false
    c. class
    d. caste

8. Which of the following were viewed by Weber as analytically distinct components of stratification?
    a. conformity, deviance, and social control
    b. class, status, and power
    c. class, caste, and age
    d. class, prestige, and esteem

9. Which sociological perspective argues that stratification is universal and that social inequality is necessary so that people will be motivated to fill socially important positions?
    a. the functionalist perspective
    b. the conflict perspective
    c. the interactionist perspective
    d. the labeling perspective

10. The intellectual tradition at the heart of conflict theory begins principally with the work of
    a. Max Weber.
    b. Émile Durkheim.
    c. Erving Goffman.
    d. Karl Marx.

11. British sociologist Ralf Dahrendorf views social classes as groups of people who share common interests resulting from their authority relationships. Dahrendorf's ideology best aligns with which theoretical perspective?
    a. functionalism
    b. conflict theory
    c. interactionism
    d. sociocultural evolution

12. The respect or admiration that an occupation holds in a society is referred to as
    a. status.
    b. esteem.
    c. prestige.
    d. ranking

13. _____ refers to the reputation that a specific person has earned within an occupation.

    a. Prestige

    b. Esteem

    c. Status

    d. Power

14. In 2001, about _____ percent of the wealth of the United States was held by the richest fifth (or top 20 percent) of the population.

    a. 23

    b. 38

    c. 85

    d. 75

15. Approximately _____ out of every nine people in this country lives below the poverty line established by the federal government.

    a. one

    b. two

    c. three

    d. four

16. _____ poverty is a floating standard of deprivation by which people at the bottom of a society, whatever their lifestyles, are judged to be disadvantaged in comparison with the nation as a whole.

    a. Absolute

    b. Relative

    c. Structural

    d. Direct

17. The fact that a doctor in the Congo has a lower standard of living than a poor man in Appalachia illustrates which idea about poverty?

    a. Even doctors are treated poorly in Africa.

    b. Welfare programs are too generous in the United States.

    c. Standards of poverty are relative.

    d. There are no job opportunities in Africa.

18.   In 2006, 42 percent of poor people in the United States were living in
    a. central cities.
    b. the suburbs.
    c. rural areas.
    d. Appalachia.

19.   Which sociologist has applied functionalist analysis to the existence of poverty and argues that various segments of society actually benefit from the existence of the poor?
    a. Émile Durkheim
    b. Max Weber
    c. Karl Marx
    d. Herbert Gans

20.   The term Max Weber used to refer to people's opportunities to provide themselves with material goods, positive living conditions, and favorable life experiences is
    a. power.
    b. wealth.
    c. life chances.
    d. the Titanic effect.

21.   The poor, minorities, and those who live in rural communities and inner cities are not as likely to have access to the Internet as other members of society in the United States. This situation is called
    a. the cybervoid.
    b. electronic redlining.
    c. the digital divide.
    d. the technology gap.

22.   Which of the following is NOT an example of a closed stratification system?
    a. slavery
    b. caste system
    c. class system
    d. *varnas*

23. *Airline pilot* and *police officer* have the same occupational prestige ranking. Suppose that a former airline pilot becomes a police officer. Sociologists call this kind of movement _____ mobility.

    a. vertical

    b. intergenerational

    c. downward

    d. horizontal

24. _____ mobility involves changes in social position within a person's adult life.

    a. Intragenerational

    b. Intergenerational

    c. Horizontal

    d. Vertical

25. A plumber whose father was a physician is an example of

    a. downward intergenerational mobility.

    b. upward intergenerational mobility.

    c. downward intragenerational mobility.

    d. upward intragenerational mobility.

FILL-IN QUESTIONS: Fill in the blank spaces in the sentences below with the correct words. Where two or more words are required, there will be a corresponding number of blank spaces.

1. _____ involves the ways in which one generation passes on social inequalities to the next, producing groups of people arranged in rank order from low to high.

2. In the _____ system of stratification, peasants were required to work land leased to them by nobles in exchange for military protection and other services.

3. Karl Marx viewed _____ differentiation as the crucial determinant of social, economic, and political inequality.

4. In Karl Marx's view, a worker who feels that he or she is being treated fairly by the bourgeoisie is guilty of _____ consciousness.

5. _____ _____ is the term Thorstein Veblen used to describe the extravagant spending patterns of those at the top of the class hierarchy.

6. _____ theorists believe that a differential system of rewards and punishments is necessary for the efficient operation of society.

7. In Karl Marx's view, a capitalist society has a(n) _____ ideology that serves the interests of the ruling class.

8. The key to the _____ method of measuring social class is that the researcher, rather than the person being classified, identifies an individual's class position.

9. From 1929 through 1970, the United States government's economic and tax policies seemed to shift income shares slightly to the _____.
    However, in the past three decades, federal tax policies have favored the
    _____.

10. One commonly used measure of absolute poverty is the federal government's _____ _____, which serves as an official definition of which people are poor.

11. Since World War II, an increasing proportion of the poor people of the United States have been women, many of whom are divorced or never-married mothers. This alarming trend is known as the _____ _____
    _____.

12. Sociologist William Julius Wilson and other social scientists have used the term _____ to describe the long-term poor who lack training and skills.

13. _____ _____ notes that it is functional for society to have poor people, because the identification and punishment of the poor as deviants upholds the legitimacy of conventional social norms and "mainstream" values regarding hard work, thrift, and honesty.

14. An open class system implies that the position of each individual is influenced by the person's _____ status.

15. A woman who enters the paid labor force as a teacher's aide and eventually becomes superintendent of the school district experiences upward _____ mobility.

UNDERSTANDING SOCIAL POLICY: Each of the following questions is based on material that appears in the social policy section on "Rethinking Welfare in North America and Europe." Write a brief answer to each question in the space provided below.

1.   What is the Personal Responsibility and Work Opportunity Reconciliation Act?

2.   Compare the commitment to social service programs in the United States with programs that exist in European nations.

3.   Why do sociologists tend to view the debate over welfare throughout industrialized nations from a conflict perspective?

DEFINITIONS OF KEY TERMS

Social inequality: A condition in which members of society have different amounts of wealth, prestige, or power.

Stratification: A structured ranking of entire groups of people that perpetuates unequal economic rewards and power in a society.

Income: Salaries and wages.

Wealth: An inclusive term encompassing all a person's material assets, including land, stocks, and other types of property.

Ascribed status: A social position assigned to a person by society without regard for the person's unique talents or characteristics.

Achieved status: A social position that a person attains largely through his or her own efforts.

Slavery: A system of enforced servitude in which some people are owned by other people.

Caste: A hereditary rank, usually religiously dictated, that tends to be fixed and immobile.

Estate system: A system of stratification under which peasants were required to work land leased to them by nobles in exchange for military protection and other services. Also known as *feudalism*.

Class system: A social ranking based primarily on economic position in which achieved characteristics can influence social mobility.

Capitalism: An economic system in which the means of production are held largely in private hands and the main incentive for economic activity is the accumulation of profits.

Bourgeoisie: Karl Marx's term for the capitalist class, comprising the owners of the means of production.

Proletariat: Karl Marx's term for the working class in a capitalist society.

Class consciousness: In Karl Marx's view, a subjective awareness held by members of a class regarding their common vested interests and need for collective political action to bring about social change.

False consciousness: A term used by Karl Marx to describe an attitude held by members of a class that does not accurately reflect their objective position.

Class: A group of people who have a similar level of wealth and income.

Status group: People who have the same prestige or lifestyle, independent of their class positions.

Power: The ability to exercise one's will over others.

Dominant ideology: A set of cultural beliefs and practices that helps to maintain powerful social, economic, and political interests.

Objective method: A technique for measuring social class that assigns individuals to classes based on criteria such as occupation, education, income, and place of residence.

Prestige: The respect and admiration that an occupation holds in a society.

Esteem: The reputation that a specific person has earned within an occupation.

Socioeconomic status (SES): A measure of social class that is based on income, education, and occupation.

Absolute poverty: A minimum level of subsistence that no family should be expected to live below.

Relative poverty: A floating standard of deprivation by which people at the bottom of a society, whatever their lifestyles, are judged to be disadvantaged *in comparison with the nation as a whole*.

Underclass: The long-term poor who lack training and skills.

Life chances: The opportunities people have to provide themselves with material goods, positive living conditions, and favorable life experiences.

Digital divide: The relative lack of access to the latest technologies among low-income groups, racial and ethnic minorities, rural residents and the citizens of developing countries.

Social mobility: Movement of individuals or groups from one position in a society's stratification system to another.

Open system: A social system in which the position of each individual is influenced by his or her achieved status.

Closed system: A social system in which there is little or no possibility of individual social mobility.

Horizontal mobility: The movement of an individual from one social position to another of the same rank.

Vertical mobility: The movement of a person from one social position to another of a different rank.

Intergenerational mobility: Changes in the social position of children relative to their parents.

Intragenerational mobility: Changes in social position within a person's adult life.

Corporate welfare: Tax breaks, direct payments, and grants that the government makes to corporations.

ANSWERS TO SELF-TEST

Modified True/False Questions

1. Although slave status in ancient Greece could be inherited by succeeding generations, it was not necessarily permanent.

2. True

3. Urbanization and technological changes have weakened the caste system in India.

4. According to Daniel Rossides, the largest social class in the United States is the working class.

5. True

6. Max Weber suggested that status can diverge from economic class standing. For example, a successful pickpocket may be in the same income class as a college professor, yet the thief is widely regarded as a member of a lower status group than that of the professor.

7. True

8. True

9. The objective method of measuring social class views class largely as a statistical category.

10. True

11. Tax policies during the past three decades have favored the affluent. As a result, the income gap has become larger.

12. True

13. True

14.   In recent years, colleges and universities have been allocating a higher proportion of financial aid in the form of low-interest students loans.

15.   Gender remains an important factor in shaping social mobility within the United States.

Multiple-Choice Questions

1.	d	10.	d	19.	d
2.	b	11.	b	20.	c
3.	a	12.	c	21.	c
4.	a	13.	b	22.	c
5.	a	14.	c	23.	d
6.	a	15.	a	24.	a
7.	c	16.	b	25.	a
8.	b	17.	c		
9.	a	18.	a		

Fill-In Questions

1.	Stratification	9.	poor; affluent
2.	estate	10.	poverty line
3.	class	11.	feminization of poverty
4.	false	12.	underclass
5.	Conspicuous consumption	13.	(Herbert) Gans
6.	Functionalist	14.	achieved
7.	dominant	15.	intragenerational
8.	objective		

Understanding Social Policy: Rethinking Welfare in North America and Europe

1.   In late 1996, in a historic shift in federal policy, Congress passed the Personal Responsibility and Work Opportunity Reconciliation Act. This law ended the long-standing federal guarantee of assistance to every poor family that meets eligibility requirements. The law set a lifetime limit of five years of welfare and required all able-bodied adults to work after receiving two years of benefits. The federal government would give block grants to the states to use as they wished in assisting poor and needy residents, and it would permit states to experiment with ways to move people off welfare.

2.   Most industrialized nations devote higher proportions of their expenditures to housing, social security, welfare, health care, and unemployment compensation than the United States does.

3.   Sociologists tend to view the debate over welfare reform in industrialized nations from a conflict perspective: The "haves" in positions of policymaking listen to the interests of other "haves," while the cries of the "have-nots" are drowned out. From a conflict perspective, the backlash against welfare recipients reflects deep fears and hostility toward the nation's urban, predominantly African American and Hispanic underclass.

9 GLOBAL INEQUALITY

The Global Divide

Stratification in the World System
  The Legacy of Colonialism
  Multinational Corporations
  Worldwide Poverty
  Modernization

Stratification within Nations: A Comparative Perspective
  Distribution of Wealth and Income
  Social Mobility

Case Study: Stratification in Mexico
  Mexico's Economy
  Race Relations in Mexico: The Color Hierarchy
  The Status of Women in Mexico
  The Borderlands

Social Policy and Global Inequality: Universal Human Rights
  The Issue
  The Setting
  Sociological Insights
  Policy Initiatives

BOXES
  SOCIOLOGY IN THE GLOBAL COMMUNITY: Cutting Poverty Worldwide
  SOCIOLOGY IN THE GLOBAL COMMUNITY: The Global Disconnect
  SOCIAL IN THE GLOBAL COMMUNITY: Stratification in Japan
  TAKING SOCIOLOGY TO WORK: Bari Katz, Program Director, National Conference of Community and Justice

KEY POINTS

The Global Divide: Around the world, inequality is a significant determinant of human behavior. Disparities in life chances across the globe are extreme. However, a few centuries ago, such vast divides in global wealth did not exist. This was true until the Industrial Revolution and rising agricultural productivity produced explosive economic growth. The resulting rise in living standards was not evenly distributed across the world.

Colonialism and Neocolonialism: **Colonialism** is the maintenance of political, social, economic, and cultural domination over a people by a foreign power for an extended period. In simple terms, it is rule by outsiders. By the 1980s, colonialism had largely disappeared. Most of the nations that were colonies before World War I had achieved political independence and established their own governments. However, their dependence on more industrialized nations—including their former colonial masters—for managerial and technical expertise, investment capital, and manufactured goods kept former colonies in a subservient position. Such continuing dependence and foreign domination constitute **neocolonialism**.

World Systems Theory and Dependency Theory: Drawing on the conflict perspective, sociologist Immanuel Wallerstein views the global economic system as being divided between nations who control wealth and those from which resources are taken. Wallerstein has advanced a **world systems analysis** to describe the unequal economic and political relationships in which certain industrialized nations (among them, the United States, Japan, and Germany) and their corporations dominate the core of the system. Wallerstein suggests that the poor developing countries of Asia, Africa, and Latin America are on the periphery of the world economic system. Core nations and their corporations control and exploit non-core nations' economies.

Globalization: Globalization is the worldwide integration of government policies, cultures, social movements, and financial markets through trade and the exchange of ideas. Some observers see globalization and its effects as the natural result of advances in communications technology. Others view it more critically, as a process that allows multinational corporations to expand unchecked.

Multinational Corporations: The term **multinational corporation** refers to commercial organizations that are headquartered in one country but do business throughout the world. Conflict theorists conclude that, on the whole, multinational corporations have a negative social impact on workers in both industrialized and developing nations. Workers in the United States and other core countries are beginning to recognize that their own interests are served by helping to organize workers in developing nations. As long as multinationals can exploit cheap labor abroad, they will be in a strong position to reduce wages and benefits in industrialized countries.

Modernization and Modernization Theory: Contemporary social scientists use the term **modernization** to describe the far-reaching process by which peripheral nations move from traditional or less developed institutions to those characteristic of more developed societies. Many sociologists are quick to note that terms such as modernization, and even development, contain an ethnocentric bias. A similar criticism has been made of **modernization theory**, a functionalist approach proposing that modernization and development will gradually improve the lives of people in developing nations. According to this theory, while countries develop at uneven rates, the development of peripheral countries will be assisted by innovations transferred from the industrialized world.

Stratification within Nations—A Comparative Perspective: At the same time that the gap between rich and poor nations is widening, so too is the gap between rich and poor citizens within developing nations. In at least 26 nations around the world, the most affluent 10 percent of the population receives at least 40 percent of all income. Women in developing countries find life especially difficult.

Comparative Social Mobility: It would be incorrect to assume that the degree of social mobility and the means for obtaining mobility are the same in all class systems. Studies of intergenerational mobility in industrial nations have found the following patterns: substantial similarities exist in the ways that parents' positions in stratification systems are transmitted to their children; mobility opportunities in other nations have been influenced by structural factors, such as labor market changes; and immigration continues to be a significant factor in shaping a society's level of intergenerational mobility. Within developing nations, micro-level movement from one occupation to another is often overshadowed by macro-level social and economic changes.

Stratification in Mexico—A Case Study: Although Mexico is unquestionably a poor country, the gap between its richest and poorest citizens is one of the widest in the world. The subordinate status of Mexico's Indians is but one reflection of the nation's color hierarchy, which links social class to the appearance of racial purity. There is widespread denial of prejudice and discrimination against people of color in Mexico. Feminist sociologists emphasize that even when Mexican women work outside the home, they often are not recognized as active and productive household members, while men are typically viewed as heads of households. Growing recognition of the borderlands reflects the increasingly close and complex relationship between Mexico and the United States.

Universal Human Rights: Poised on the third millennium, the world seemed capable of mighty feats, yet at the same time came constant reminders of how quickly people and their fundamental human rights could be trampled. **Human rights** refers to universal moral rights possessed by all people because they are human. The most important elaboration of human rights appears in the Universal Declaration of Human Rights, adopted by the United Nations in 1948. This declaration prohibits slavery, torture, and degrading punishment; grants everyone the right to a nationality and its culture; affirms freedom of religion and the right to vote; proclaims the right to seek asylum in other countries to escape persecution; and prohibits arbitrary interference with one's privacy and arbitrary taking of a person's property. Cultural relativism encourages understanding and respecting the distinctive norms, values, and customs of each culture. In some situations, conflicts arise between human rights standards and local social practices that rest on alternative views of human dignity. Conflict theorists would point out how much more quickly we become embroiled in "human rights" concerns when oil is at stake, or when military alliances come into play. In addition to the United Nations, non-governmental organizations (NGOs) such as Médecins sans Frontières and Amnesty International have become human rights watchdogs.

KEY TERMS

Briefly define or identify the following terms in the spaces provided below. The definitions of these terms can be found later in this chapter of the study guide.

Colonialism	Modernization
Neocolonialism	Gross national product
World systems analysis	Modernization theory
Dependency theory	Borderlands
Globalization	Remittances
Multinational corporation	Human rights

SELF-TEST

MODIFIED TRUE/FALSE QUESTIONS: If the statement below is true, write "true" in the space provided. If the statement is false, briefly correct the error.

1.   The lifestyles portrayed in the media in countries like India are out of reach economically for all but a small percentage of the population.

2.   Current trends show that the average value of goods and services produced per citizen in the industrialized nations was equivalent to that of poorer countries.

3.   The global debt crisis has lessened the Third World dependency begun under colonialism, neocolonialism, and multinational investment.

4.   In the developing world, it is easy to build strong trade unions in factories run by multinational corporations.

5.   Several sociologists who have surveyed the effects of foreign investment by multinationals conclude that, although it may initially contribute to a host nation's wealth, it eventually increases economic inequality within developing nations.

6.   The main implication of the global disconnect is that people in "disconnected" countries are unable to play Internet games or surf the Web.

7.   Many contemporary researchers view modernization as movement along a series of social indicators—among them, degree of urbanization, energy use, literacy, mass transit systems, political democracy, and use of birth control.

8.   Karuna Chanana Ahmed, an anthropologist from India who has studied developing nations, calls Blacks the most exploited among oppressed people.

9.   Japan's level of income inequality is among the highest of major industrial societies.

10.   More than 25 percent of Japanese women in the work force hold management positions.

11.   Cross-cultural studies suggest that intragenerational mobility has been increasing in recent decades, at least among men.

12.   Since the 1960s there has been a close cultural, economic, and political relationship between Mexico and the United States.

13.   Gross national income is a commonly used measure of an average resident's economic well-being.

14.   As far back as 1973, women in Monterrey—Mexico's third largest city—began protesting the continuing disruptions of the city's water supply. Their efforts brought improvement in water service, but the issue of reliable and safe water remains a concern.

15.   *Maquiladoras* are foreign factories established just across the border in Mexico. They do not have to pay taxes, and they are not required to provide insurance or benefits for their workers.

MULTIPLE-CHOICE QUESTIONS: Read each question carefully and then select the best answer.

1.   In viewing the global economic system as divided between nations that control wealth and those from which capital is taken, sociologist Immanuel Wallerstein draws on the
        a. functionalist perspective.
        b. conflict perspective.
        c. interactionist perspective.
        d. dramaturgical approach.

2.   Which of the following is NOT one of the components of Wallerstein's world systems theory?
        a. the core
        b. the dependent
        c. the semiperiphery
        d. the periphery

3.   Which of the following nations would Wallerstein classify as a core country within the world economic system?
        a. Germany
        b. South Korea
        c. Ireland
        d. Mexico

4.   Which of the following nations would Wallerstein classify as on the periphery of the world economic system?

      a. Germany

      b. South Korea

      c. Ireland

      d. Mexico

5.   Sociologist Immanuel Wallerstein's method of analysis is the most widely used version of which theory?

      a. functionalism

      b. conflict theory

      c. dependency theory

      d. interactionism

6.   The term _____ refers to commercial organizations that are headquartered in one country but do business throughout the world.

      a. world systems

      b. multinational corporations

      c. interlocking directorates

      d. top-down management

7.   The term global factory refers to

      a. a particular type of postindustrial organization.

      b. interlocking directorates.

      c. factories throughout the world run by multinational corporations.

      d. modernization.

8.   The _____ perspective argues that multinational corporations can actually help the developing nations of the world.

      a. interactionist

      b. feminist

      c. functionalist

      d. conflict

9.   Which sociological perspective emphasizes that multinational corporations exploit local workers to maximize profits?
    a. the functionalist perspective
    b. the conflict perspective
    c. the interactionist perspective
    d. labeling theory

10.   According to a ranking by revenues, the largest industrial company in the world is
    a. Wal-Mart.
    b. International Business Machines (IBM).
    c. General Motors.
    d. Mitsubishi.

11.   In a map of the world drawn to reflect the number of poor people in each country, which of these areas would be the smallest?
    a. Africa
    b. China
    c. India
    d. the United States

12.   About how many of the world's people live on less than two dollars a day?
    a. 10 million
    b. 100 million
    c. 3 billion
    d. 5 billion

13.   Modernization theory is associated with
    a. the functionalist perspective.
    b. the conflict perspective.
    c. the interactionist perspective.
    d. labeling theory.

14.   Current modernization studies generally take a _____ perspective. Using various indicators, researchers show how societies are moving closer together despite traditional differences.
    a. dependency
    b. convergence
    c. labeling
    d. world systems

15. In one example of social stratification, the Japanese find it difficult to sit, talk, or eat together unless the relative rankings of those present have been established, often through the practice of _____, or the exchange of business cards.
    a. pokéman
    b. *meishi*
    c. *varnas*
    d. hara-kiri

16. The Japanese minority group known as the *Burakumin* constitutes a low-status
    a. subculture.
    b. counterculture.
    c. neocolonialism.
    d. in-group.

17. Mobility patterns in industrialized countries are usually associated with
    a. intergenerational mobility.
    b. positive mobility.
    c. intragenerational mobility.
    d. both a and c

18. Which of the following nations has the largest gap in income between its most affluent and least affluent residents?
    a. Brazil
    b. Jamaica
    c. Sweden
    d. the United States

19. Since the early twentieth century, the United States and Mexico have had a close _____ relationship.
    a. cultural
    b. economic
    c. political
    d. all of the above

20. Which of the following terms refers to Mexico's large, impoverished majority, most of whom have brown skin and a mixed racial lineage due to intermarriage?
    a. *criollo*
    b. *indio*
    c. *mestizo*
    d. *Zapatista*

21. In Mexico, women now constitute _____ percent of the labor force.
    a. 15
    b. 23
    c. 35
    d. 42

22. The area of a common culture along the border between Mexico and the United States is referred to as the
    a. wetback line.
    b. borderlands.
    c. illegal aliens line.
    d. *maquiladoras.*

23. Which perspective would view immigration into the United States from Mexico as a labor-market issue, and would emphasize that this is another example of a core industrialized nation exploiting a peripheral developing country?
    a. modernization theory
    b. labeling theory
    c. world systems theory
    d. anomie theory

24. Which of the following is NOT included in the Universal Declaration of Human Rights, as adopted by the United Nations in 1948?
    a. the prohibition of slavery, torture, and degrading punishment
    b. the right of an individual to seek his or her self-interests in a capitalistic fashion
    c. the right to a nationality and its culture
    d. the prohibition of the arbitrary interference with one's privacy

25. During the 1990s, within the former Yugoslavia, Serbs initiated a policy intended to remove Muslims from parts of Bosnia-Herzegovina and ethnic Albanians from the province of Kosovo. These actions brought the term _____ into the world's vocabulary
    a. infanticide
    b. geronticide
    c. mercy killing
    d. ethnic cleansing

FILL-IN QUESTIONS: Fill in the blank spaces in the sentences below with the correct words. Where two or more words are required, there will be a corresponding number of blank spaces.

1. The long reign of the British Empire over much of North America, parts of Africa, and India is an example of _____ domination.

2. When two countries have a(n) _____ relationship, the dependence of a former colony on more industrialized nations for managerial and technical expertise, investment capital, and manufactured goods keeps it in a subservient position.

3. In a sense, dependency theory can be regarded as an application of the _____ perspective on a global scale.

4. As _____ industries become a more important part of the international marketplace, many companies have concluded that the low costs of overseas operations more than offset the expense of transmitting information around the world.

5. Viewed from a(n) _____ perspective, the combination of skilled technology and management provided by multinationals and the relatively cheap labor available in developing nations is ideal for a global enterprise.

6. Members of societies that have undergone modernization shift allegiance from _____ sources of authority such as parents and priests to newer authorities such as government officials.

7. The technological disconnect between developing and industrial nations is known as the _____ _____.

8. Many sociologists are quick to note that terms such as modernization and development contain a(n) _____ bias.

9. In 1985, Japan's parliament passed an equal employment bill that encourages employers to end _____ discrimination in hiring, assignment, and promotion policies.

10. Cross-cultural studies of industrial nations suggest that intergenerational mobility has been increasing in recent decades, at least among _____.

11. According to _____'s analysis, the United States is at the core, whereas neighboring Mexico is still on the semiperiphery of the world economic system.

12. Every year, hundreds of Mexicans die as they try to cross the border into the _____ _____.

13. _____ _____ _____ is a commonly used measure of an average resident's economic well-being.

14. About _____ percent of adults in the United States have a high school education, compared to only _____ percent of those in Mexico.

15. Many Mexicans who have come to the United States send some part of their earnings back across the border to family members still in Mexico. This substantial flow of money is sometimes referred to as remittances or "_____."

UNDERSTANDING SOCIAL POLICY: Each of the following questions is based on material that appears in the social policy section on "Universal Human Rights." Write a brief answer to each question in the space provided below.

1. What is the Universal Declaration of Human Rights?

2. In what way(s) is the sociological concept of cultural relativism relevant to the human rights issue?

3. How would functionalists approach the issue of universal human rights?

DEFINITIONS OF KEY TERMS

Colonialism: The maintenance of political, social, economic, and cultural dominance over a people by a foreign power for an extended period.

Neocolonialism: Continuing dependence of former colonies on foreign countries.

World systems analysis: A view of the global economic system as one divided between certain industrialized nations that control wealth and developing countries that are controlled and exploited.

Dependency theory: An approach that contends that industrialized nations continue to exploit developing countries for their own gain.

Globalization: The emergence of worldwide markets and communications that increasingly ignore national boundaries.

Multinational corporation: A commercial organization that is headquartered in one country but does business throughout the world.

Gross National Product (GNP): The value of a nation's goods and products.

Modernization: The far-reaching process by which periphery nations move from traditional or less developed institutions to those characteristic of more developed societies.

Modernization theory: A functionalist approach that proposes that modernization and development will gradually improve the lives of people in developing nations.

Borderlands: The area of common culture along the border between Mexico and the United States.

Remittances: The monies that immigrants return to their families of origin. Also called *migradollars*.

Human Rights: Universal moral rights possessed by all people because they are human.

ANSWERS TO SELF-TEST

Modified True/False Questions

1. True
2. In 2004, the average value of goods and services produced per citizen in the United States, Japan, Switzerland, Belgium, and Norway was more than $30,000. In at least twelve poorer countries, the value was $900 or less.
3. The global debt crisis has intensified the Third World dependency begun under colonialism, neocolonialism, and multinational investment.
4. In the developing world, it is difficult to build strong trade unions in factories run by multinational corporations.
5. True
6. Becoming integrated into the global economy is not possible without access to the Internet.
7. Mass transit is not one of the social indicators that determines modernity.
8. Karuna Chanana Ahmed calls women the most exploited among oppressed people.
9. Japan's level of income inequality is among the lowest of major industrial societies.
10. Only about 10 percent of Japan's managers are female.
11. Cross-cultural studies suggest that intergenerational mobility has been increasing in recent decades, at least among men.
12. Since the early 20th century there has been a close cultural, economic, and political relationship between Mexico and the United States.
13. True
14. True
15. True

Multiple-Choice Questions

1.	b	10.	a	19.	d
2.	b	11.	d	20.	c
3.	a	12.	c	21.	d
4.	d	13.	a	22.	b
5.	c	14.	b	23.	c
6.	b	15.	b	24.	b
7.	c	16.	a	25.	d
8.	c	17.	a		
9.	b	18.	a		

Fill-In Questions

1.	colonial	9.	sex
2.	neocolonial	10.	men
3.	conflict	11.	Wallerstein
4.	service	12.	United States
5.	functionalist	13.	Gross national income
6.	traditional	14.	87; 13
7.	global disconnect	15.	*migradollars*
8.	ethnocentric		

Understanding Social Policy: Universal Human Rights

1. The Universal Declaration of Human Rights, adopted by the United Nations in 1948, prohibits slavery, torture, and degrading punishment; grants everyone the right to a nationality and its culture; affirms freedom of religion and the right to vote; proclaims the right to seek asylum in other countries to escape persecution; and prohibits arbitrary interference with one's privacy and arbitrary taking of a person's property. It also emphasizes that mothers and children are entitled to special care and assistance.

2. Cultural relativism encourages the understanding and respect for the distinctive norms, values, and customs of each culture. In some situations, conflicts arise between human rights standards and local social practices that rest on alternative views of human dignity.

3. Conflict theorists would point out how much more quickly we become embroiled in "human rights" concerns when oil is at stake, as in the Middle East, or when military alliances come into play, as in Europe. Governments ratify human rights but resist independent efforts to enforce them within their own borders.

10 RACIAL AND ETHNIC INEQUALITY

Minority, Racial, and Ethnic Groups
> Minority Groups
> Race
> Ethnicity

Prejudice and Discrimination
> Prejudice
> Color-Blind Racism
> Discriminatory Behavior
> The Privileges of the Dominant
> Institutional Discrimination

Sociological Perspectives on Race and Ethnicity
> Functionalist Perspective
> Conflict Perspective
> Interactionist Perspective

Patterns of Intergroup Relations
> Amalgamation
> Assimilation
> Segregation
> Pluralism

Race and Ethnicity in the United States
> Racial Groups
> Ethnic Groups

Social Policy and Racial and Ethnic Inequality: Racial Profiling
> The Issue
> The Setting
> Sociological Insights
> Policy Initiatives

BOXES
> **TAKING SOCIOLOGY TO WORK**: Prudence Hannis: Liason Officer, National Institute of Science Research, University of Québec
> **RESEARCH TODAY**: Interracial and Interethnic Friendships
> **SOCIOLOGY ON CAMPUS**: Asian-American Diversity
> **RESEARCH TODAY**: Social Mobility Among Latino Immigrants

KEY POINTS

Racial and Ethnic Groups: Sociologists frequently distinguish between racial groups and ethnic groups. The term **racial group** is used to describe a group that is set apart from others because of physical differences that have taken on social significance. Whites, African Americans, and Asian Americans are all considered racial groups in the United States. Unlike racial groups, an **ethnic group** is set apart from others primarily because of its national origin or distinctive cultural patterns. In the United States, Puerto Ricans, Jews, and Polish Americans are all categorized as ethnic groups.

Minority Groups: A **minority group** is a subordinate group whose members have significantly less control or power over their own lives than members of a dominant or majority group have over theirs. Sociologists have identified five basic properties of a minority group: (1) Members experience treatment that is unequal to the treatment of those in the majority; (2) members share physical or cultural characteristics that distinguish them from the dominant group; (3) membership in the group is not voluntary; people are born into the group; (4) minority group members have a strong sense of group solidarity; and (5) members generally marry others from the same group.

Prejudice: **Prejudice** is a negative attitude toward an entire category of people, often an ethnic or racial minority. One important and widespread form of prejudice is **racism**, the belief that one race is supreme and that all others are innately inferior. When racism prevails in a society, members of subordinate groups generally experience prejudice, discrimination, and exploitation.

Studying Race and Ethnicity: Viewing race from the macro level, functionalists observe that racial prejudice and discrimination serve positive functions for dominant groups, whereas conflict theorists see the economic structure as a central factor in the exploitation of minorities. The micro-level analysis of interactionist researchers stresses the manner in which everyday contact between people from different racial and ethnic backgrounds contributes to tolerance or leads to hostility.

Racial Profiling: Racial profiling is any police-initiated action based on race, ethnicity, or national origin rather than on a person's behavior. Generally, profiling occurs when law enforcement officers, including customs officials, airport security personnel, and police, assume that people who fit certain descriptions are likely to engage in illegal activities.

Patterns of Intergroup Relations: There are four identifiable patterns that describe typical intergroup relations. **Amalgamation** describes the result when a majority group and a minority group combine to form a new group. Through intermarriage over several generations, various groups in society combine to form a new group. **Assimilation** is the process through which a person forsakes his or her own cultural tradition to become part of a different culture. Generally, it is practiced by a minority group member who wants to conform to the standards of the dominant group. **Segregation** refers to the physical separation of two groups of people in terms of residence, workplace, and social events. Generally, a dominant group imposes this pattern on a minority group. **Pluralism** is based on mutual respect between various groups in a society for one another's cultures. This pattern allows a minority group to express its own culture, and still participate without prejudice in the larger society.

African Americans: Despite their large numbers, African Americans have long been treated as second-class citizens. Currently, by the standards of the federal government, more than 1 out of every 4 Blacks—as opposed to 1 out of every 12 Whites—is poor. Contemporary institutional discrimination and individual prejudice against African Americans are rooted in the history of slavery in the United States. During the 1960s, a vast civil rights movement emerged with many competing factions and strategies for change. Some African Americans—especially middle-class men and women—have made economic gains over the last 50 years.

Native Americans: There are approximately 2.5 million Native Americans in the United States. They represent a diverse array of cultures, distinguishable by language, family organization, religion, and livelihood. Today, life remains difficult for members of the 554 tribal groups in the United States, whether they live in cities or on reservations. By the 1990s, an increasing number of people in the United States were openly claiming a Native American identity. Since 1960, the federal government's count of Native Americans has tripled, to an estimated 2.5 million.

Asian Americans: Asian Americans are held up as a **model** or **ideal minority** group, supposedly because despite past suffering from prejudice and discrimination, they have succeeded economically, socially, and educationally without resorting to confrontations with Whites. This concept of a model minority ignores the diversity among Asian Americans. There are rich and poor Japanese Americans, rich and poor Filipino Americans, and so forth. The existence of a model minority seems to reaffirm the notion that anyone can get ahead in the United States with talent and hard work, and implies that those minorities that don't succeed are somehow responsible for their failures. Viewed from a conflict perspective, this attitude is yet another instance of "blaming the victims."

Arab Americans: Arab Americans are immigrants and their descendents who hail from the 22 nations of the Arab world, located in North Africa and the Middle East. By some estimates, up to 3 million people of Arab ancestry reside in the United States. Despite the stereotype, most Arab Americans are not Muslim, and not all practice religion. Despite their great diversity, profiling of potential terrorists at airports has put Arab and Muslim Americans under special surveillance.

Latinos—An Overview: The various groups included under the general category "Latino" represent the largest minority in the United States. The various Latino groups share a heritage of Spanish language and culture, which can cause serious problems in their assimilation. The educational difficulties of Latino students contribute to the generally low economic status of Hispanics.

Jewish Americans: Jews have not achieved equality in the United States. Despite high levels of education and professional training, they are still conspicuously absent from the top management of large corporations (except for the few firms founded by Jews). A 1994 tabulation by the Anti-Defamation League (ADL) indicated that in that year anti-Semitic acts had reached their highest level of the previous 19 years in which the ADL had been recording such incidents. As is true for other minorities, Jewish Americans face choosing between maintaining ties to their long religious and cultural heritage or becoming as indistinguishable as possible from gentiles.

Global Immigration: Worldwide immigration is at an all time high. Many immigrants are transnationals, people who move across borders many times in search of jobs and education. Functionalists point out that immigrants adapt to the new society and become assets to the economy by alleviating labor shortages, while remittances help the country of origin. Conflict theorists note that racial and ethnic hostilities can be hidden in arguments about the economics of immigration. Feminists observe that immigrant women face economic hardship as well as the stress of negotiating the new system on behalf of their children. In the U.S. increased public perception that the U.S. has lost control of its borders has led to increased pressure for immigration control. Terrorist attacks of 2001 caused increased government scrutiny of immigrants as they attempt to travel to many nations.

KEY TERMS

Briefly define or identify the following terms in the spaces provided below. The definitions of these terms can be found later in this chapter of the study guide.

Racial group	Racism
Ethnic group	Hate crime
Minority group	Color-blind racism

Racial formation	Discrimination
Stereotype	Glass ceiling
Prejudice	Institutional discrimination
Ethnocentrism	Affirmative action
Exploitation theory	Pluralism
Contact hypothesis	Black power
Genocide	Model or ideal minority
Amalgamation	Anti-Semitism
Assimilation	Symbolic ethnicity
Segregation	Racial profiling
Apartheid	

SELF-TEST

MODIFIED TRUE/FALSE QUESTIONS: If the statement below is true, write "true" in the space provided. If the statement is false, briefly correct the error.

1. When sociologists define a minority group, they are primarily concerned with the economic and political power, or powerlessness, of that group.

2. The one-drop rule was a vivid example of the biological construction of race.

3. When allowed to check off multiple racial categories on the 2000 census, nearly 7 million people reported that they were of two or more races.

4. Stratification along racial lines is less resistant to change than stratification along ethnic lines.

5. A White corporate president with a completely respectful view of Vietnamese Americans refuses to hire Vietnamese Americans for executive posts out of fear that biased clients will take their business elsewhere. The president's action constitutes prejudice without discrimination.

6. In early 1995, the federal Glass Ceiling Commission found that affirmative action has completely eliminated glass ceilings and has allowed women and minority group men to win a significant proportion of top management positions in the nation's industries.

7. A rule requiring that only English be spoken at a place of work—even when it is not a business necessity—is an example of institutional discrimination.

8.   Affirmative action refers to hiring women and minorities for job openings and admitting members of these groups to college regardless of their competency.

9.   Both the enslavement of Blacks and the extermination and removal westward of Native Americans were, to a significant extent, economically motivated.

10.   The term genocide has been used in reference to the killing of 1 million Armenians by Turkey beginning in 1915.

11.   Great Britain is an example of a nation that has been notably successful in achieving cultural pluralism in a multiracial society.

12.   During World War II, the federal government decreed that all German Americans on the East Coast leave their homes and report to "evacuation camps."

13.   Arab Americans and Muslims are two different names for the same social group.

14.   Politically, Puerto Ricans in the United States have been more successful than Mexican Americans in organizing for their rights.

15.   Despite high levels of education and professional training, Jewish Americans are still conspicuously absent from the top management of large corporations (except for the few firms founded by Jews).

MULTIPLE-CHOICE QUESTIONS: Read each question carefully and then select the best answer.

1.   Which sociologist, writing in 1906, noted that individuals make distinctions between members of their own group (the in-group) and everyone else (the out-group)?
      a. Charles Horton Cooley
      b. Émile Durkheim
      c. William I. Thomas
      d. William Graham Sumner

2.   Sociologists have identified five basic properties of a minority group. Which of the following is NOT one of these properties?
      a. unequal treatment
      b. physical traits
      c. ascribed status
      d. cultural bias

3.   The largest racial minority group in the United States is
      a. Asians Americans.
      b. African Americans.
      c. Native Americans.
      d. Jewish Americans.

4.   Which of the following is considered a racial group?
      a. Irish Americans
      b. Jewish Americans
      c. African Americans
      d. all of the above

5.   Which of the following is considered an ethnic group?
      a. Puerto Ricans
      b. Jews
      c. Polish Americans
      d. all of the above

6.   What term do sociologists use to refer to a negative attitude toward an entire category of people, often an ethnic or racial minority?

    a. ethnocentrism

    b. discrimination

    c. prejudice

    d. contact hypothesis

7.   Racism is a form of

    a. ethnocentrism.

    b. discrimination.

    c. prejudice.

    d. both b and c

8.   In 2004, more than 7,400 hate crimes were reported to authorities. More than half those crimes involved

    a. ethnic bias.

    b. racial bias.

    c. religious bias.

    d. bias against sexual orientation.

9.   The term _____ refers to an invisible barrier that blocks the promotion of a qualified individual in a work environment because of that person's gender, race, or ethnicity.

    a. glass ceiling

    b. institutional discrimination

    c. affirmative action

    d. contact hypothesis

10.   Suppose that a work place requires that only English be spoken, even when it is not a business necessity to restrict the use of other languages. This would be an example of:

    a. prejudice.

    b. scapegoating.

    c. a self-fulfilling prophecy.

    d. institutional discrimination.

11. _____ refers to making positive efforts to recruit minority members or women for jobs, promotions, and educational opportunities.

    a. Institutional discrimination

    b. Amalgamation

    c. Apartheid

    d. Affirmative action

12. Which sociological perspective sees the economic structure as a central factor in the exploitation of minority groups?

    a. the functionalist perspective

    b. the conflict perspective

    c. the interactionist perspective

    d. labeling theory

13. A Hispanic woman and a Jewish man, working together as computer programmers for an electronics firm, overcome their initial prejudices and come to appreciate each other's strengths and talents. This is an example of

    a. the contact hypothesis.

    b. a self-fulfilling prophecy.

    c. amalgamation.

    d. reverse discrimination.

14. Intermarriage over several generations which results in various groups combining to form a new group would be an example of

    a. amalgamation.

    b. assimilation.

    c. segregation.

    d. pluralism.

15. Which equation can be used to represent amalgamation?

    a. $A + B + C = A$

    b. $A + B + C = A + B + C$

    c. $A + B + C = D$

    d. $A + B + C = A + B + D$

16.   What term is used to describe the process through which a person forsakes his or her cultural tradition to become a part of a different culture?

       a. amalgamation

       b. assimilation

       c. segregation

       d. pluralism

17.   Which equation can be used to represent pluralism?

       a. $A + B + C = A$

       b. $A + B + C = A + B + C$

       c. $A + B + C = D$

       d. $A + B + C = A + B + D$

18.   Who wrote the acclaimed novel *Invisible Man*?

       a. Malcolm X

       b. James Baldwin

       c. Alice Walker

       d. Ralph Ellison

19.   The approximately 2.5 million Native Americans represent a diverse array of cultures distinguishable by

       a. language.

       b. family organization.

       c. religion.

       d. all of the above

20.   Which of the following statements about Native Americans and commercial gambling is NOT true?

       a. Reservation casinos are tribally owned enterprises, and most are operated by Native Americans.

       b. Most of the gamblers who patronize Native American gaming enterprises are not Native American themselves.

       c. Even on reservations that benefit from gambling, unemployment levels are substantially higher than for the nation as a whole.

       d. About one-third of recognized Indian tribes are involved in gambling ventures.

21. The "model minority" stereotype of Asian Americans contains an implicit critique of Blacks, Hispanics, and other groups for failing to succeed as well as the model minority has. Which sociological perspective would view this as yet another instance of "blaming the victim?"
    a. functionalist perspective
    b. conflict perspective
    c. interactionist perspective
    d. dramaturgical approach

22. Which of the following statements is NOT true of Arab Americans?
    a. Arab Americans are immigrants and their descendants who hail from the 22 nations of the Arab world.
    b. The Arabic language is the single most unifying force among Arabs, although not all Arab Americans can read and speak Arabic.
    c. The most common country of origin is Lebanon.
    d. Most Arab Americans are practicing Muslims.

23. The largest Latino population of the United States is
    a. Mexican Americans.
    b. Puerto Ricans.
    c. Cuban Americans.
    d. refugees from Central America.

24. Which country has the world's largest concentration of Jews?
    a. Israel
    b. Russia
    c. the United States
    d. Poland

25. The largest population of White ethnics in the United States consists of
    a. Italian Americans.
    b. Irish Americans.
    c. Polish Americans.
    d. German Americans.

FILL-IN QUESTIONS: Fill in the blank spaces in the sentences below with the correct words. Where two or more words are required, there will be a corresponding number of blank spaces.

1. Writing from the _____ perspective, sociologist William I. Thomas observed that people respond not only to the objective features of a situation or person, but also to the meaning that situation or person has for them.

2. A(n) _____ person judges other cultures by the standards of his or her own group, which leads quite easily to prejudice against cultures viewed as inferior.

3. When White Americans can use credit cards without suspicion and browse through stores without being shadowed by security guards, they are enjoying _____ _____.

4. Sociologists such as Oliver Cox and Robert Blauner have used the _____ theory to explain the basis of racial subordination in the United States.

5. The micro-level analysis of the _____ perspective stresses the manner in which everyday contact between people from different racial and ethnic backgrounds contributes to tolerance or leads to hostility.

6. The contact hypothesis states that in _____ _____, interracial contact between people of equal status will lead to a reduction in prejudice.

7. In the United States, there are Italian Americans, Polish Americans, Hispanics, and Jews who have changed their names to those typically found among White, Protestant families. This is an example of _____.

8. In 1994, a prominent Black activist, _____ _____, was elected as South Africa's president in the nation's first election in which Blacks were allowed to vote.

9. Over the past 40 years, new immigrants to the United States have come primarily from _____ _____, _____, and _____.

10.   The "_____ _____" laws of the southern United States, designed to enforce official segregation, were upheld as constitutional by the U.S. Supreme Court in 1896.

11.   In the 1960s, proponents of _____ _____ rejected the goal of assimilation into White, middle-class society. They defended the beauty and dignity of Black and African cultures and supported the creation of Black-controlled political and economic institutions.

12.   One _____ American teenager in six has attempted suicide—a rate four times higher than the rate for other teenagers.

13.   During the 1992 Los Angeles riots, small businesses owned by _____ Americans were a particular target.

14.   Despite the stereotype, most Arab Americans are not _____.

15.   White ethnic and racial minorities have often been antagonistic to one another because of economic competition, an interpretation in line with the _____ approach to sociology.

UNDERSTANDING SOCIAL POLICY: Each of the following questions is based on material that appears in the social policy section on "Global Immigration." Write a brief answer to each question in the space provided below.

1.   Who are transnationals and how are they different from former immigrants?

2.   Why can the U.S. expect to see increasing proportions of immigrants from Latin America and Asia?

3.   What was the impact of the 2001 terrorist attacks on immigration?

DEFINITIONS OF KEY TERMS

Racial group: A group that is set apart from others because of physical differences that have taken on a social significance.

Ethnic group: A group that is set apart from others primarily because of its national origin or distinctive cultural patterns.

Minority group: A subordinate group whose members have significantly less control or power over their lives than the members of a dominant or majority group have over theirs.

Racial formation: Sociohistorical process in which categories are created, inhibited, transformed and destroyed.

Stereotype: An unreliable generalization about all members of a group that does not recognize individual differences within the group.

Prejudice: A negative attitude toward an entire category of people, often an ethnic or racial minority.

Ethnocentrism: The tendency to assume that one's culture and way of life represent the norm or are superior to all others.

Racism: The belief that one race is supreme and that all others are innately inferior.

Hate crime: A criminal offense committed because of the offender's bias against a race, religion, ethnic group, national origin, or sexual orientation.

Color-blind racism: The use of race neutral principles to defend a socially unequal status quo.

Discrimination: The denial of opportunities and equal rights to individuals and groups because of prejudice or other arbitrary reasons.

Glass ceiling: An invisible barrier that blocks the promotion of a qualified individual in a work environment because of the individual's gender, race, or ethnicity.

Institutional discrimination: The denial of opportunities and equal rights to individuals or groups that results from the normal operations of a society.

Affirmative action: Positive efforts to recruit minority group members or women for jobs, promotions, and educational opportunities.

Exploitation theory: A Marxist theory that views racial subordination in the United States as a manifestation of the class system inherent in capitalism.

 Racial profiling: Any police-initiated action based on race, ethnicity, or national origin rather than on a person's behavior.

Contact hypothesis: An interactionist perspective which states that in cooperative circumstances, interracial contact between people of equal status will reduce prejudice.

Genocide: The deliberate, systematic killing of an entire people or nation.

Amalgamation: The process through which a majority group and a minority group combine to form a new group.

Assimilation: The process through which a person forsakes his or her own cultural tradition to become part of a different culture.

Segregation: The physical separation of two groups of people in terms of residence, workplace, and social events; often imposed on a minority group by a dominant group.

Apartheid: A former policy of the South African government, designed to maintain the separation of Blacks and other non-Whites from the dominant Whites.

Pluralism: Mutual respect for one another's cultures among the various groups in a society, which allows minorities to express their own cultures without experiencing prejudice.

Black power: A political philosophy, promoted by many younger Blacks in the 1960s, that supported the creation of Black-controlled political and economic institutions.

Model or **ideal minority**: A minority group that despite past prejudice and discrimination, succeeds economically, socially, and educationally without resorting to confrontations with Whites.

Anti-Semitism: Anti-Jewish prejudice.

Symbolic ethnicity: An ethnic identity that emphasizes concerns such as ethnic food or political issues rather than deeper ties to one's heritage.

ANSWERS TO SELF-TEST

Modified True/False Questions

1. True
2. The one-drop rule was a vivid example of the social construction of race.
3. True
4. Stratification along racial lines is more resistant to change than stratification along ethnic lines.
5. The president's action constitutes discrimination without prejudice.
6. In early 1995, the federal Glass Ceiling Commission found that glass ceilings continue to block women and minority group men from top management positions in the nation's industries.
7. True
8. Affirmative action refers to positive efforts to recruit minority members or women for jobs, promotions, and educational opportunities.
9. True
10. True

11.   Great Britain is an example of a nation that has had difficulty achieving cultural pluralism in a multiracial society.

12.   During World War II, the federal government decreed that all Japanese Americans on the West Coast leave their homes and report to "evacuation camps."

13.   While these groups overlap, many Arab Americans are Christians, and many Muslims are non-Arabs.

14.   Politically, Puerto Ricans in the United States have not been as successful as Mexican Americans in organizing for their rights.

15.   True

Multiple-Choice Questions

1.	d	10.	d	19.	d
2.	d	11.	d	20.	a
3.	b	12.	b	21.	b
4.	c	13.	a	22.	d
5.	d	14.	a	23.	a
6.	c	15.	c	24.	c
7.	c	16.	b	25.	d
8.	b	17.	b		
9.	a	18.	d		

Fill-In Questions

1.	interactionist	9.	Latin America; India; Asia
2.	ethnocentric	10.	Jim Crow
3.	White privilege	11.	Black power
4.	exploitation	12.	Native
5.	interactionist	13.	Korean
6.	cooperative circumstances	14.	Muslim
7.	assimilation	15.	conflict
8.	Nelson Mandela		

Understanding Social Policy: Global Immigration

1.   Transnationals are people who may cross national borders several times in their search for better jobs and opportunities. Some transnationals hold dual citizenship. They are less likely to develop strong loyalty to the destination country.

2.   U.S. immigration policy favors skilled laborers and the family members of U.S. residents. Over the last 40 years, immigration from Asia and Latin America have outpaced immigration from European nations, so we can expect increasing numbers of family members from those areas to seek residence in the U. S.

3.   Worldwide concerns about terrorism were heightened after the terrorist attacks of September 11, 2001. Legal and illegal immigration has come under more intense scrutiny. The wait for approval to enter has increased for potential immigrants to many nations.

CHAPTER

11

STRATIFICATION BY GENDER

Social Construction of Gender
   Gender Roles in the United States
   Cross-Cultural Perspective

Sociological Perspectives on Gender
   The Functionalist View
   The Conflict Response
   The Feminist Perspective
   The Interactionist Approach

Women: The Oppressed Majority
   Sexism and Sex Discrimination
   The Status of Women Worldwide

Women in the Workforce of the United States
   Labor Force Participation
   Compensation
   Social Consequences of Women's Employment

Emergence of a Collective Consciousness

Social Policy and Gender Stratification: The Battle over Abortion from a Global Perspective

BOXES
   RESEARCH TODAY: *Gender Roles and Volunteer Work*
   SOCIOLOGY IN THE GLOBAL COMMUNITY: *The Head Scarf and the Veil: Complex Symbols*
   TAKING SOCIOLOGY TO WORK: *Abigail E. Drevs, Former Program and Volunteer Coordinator, Y-ME Illinois*

KEY POINTS

Social Construction of Gender: In studying gender, sociologists are interested in the gender-role socialization that leads females and males to behave differently. The application of dominant gender roles leads to many forms of differentiation between women and men. Gender roles are evident not only in our work and behavior but in how we react to others. We are constantly "doing gender" without realizing it. We construct our behavior socially to create or exaggerate male-female differences.

Gender-Role Socialization in the United States: According to traditional gender-role patterns that have been influential in the socialization of children in the United States, boys must be masculine—active, aggressive, tough, daring, and dominant—but girls must be feminine—soft, emotional, sweet, and submissive. It is adults, of course, who play a critical role in guiding children into those gender roles deemed appropriate in a society. Parents are normally the first and most crucial agents of socialization. But other adults, older siblings, the mass media, and religious and educational institutions also exert an important influence on gender-role socialization in the United States and elsewhere.

The Functionalist View of Gender Stratification: Functionalists maintain that gender differentiation has contributed to overall social stability. Sociologists Talcott Parsons and Robert Bales argued that in order to function most effectively, the family requires adults who specialize in particular roles. They contended that women take the expressive, emotionally supportive role, and men take the instrumental, practical role, with the two roles complementing each other. Parsons and Bales did not explicitly endorse traditional gender roles, but they implied that a division of tasks between spouses is functional for the family as a unit.

The Conflict View of Gender Stratification: Conflict theorists see gender differences as a reflection of the subjugation of one group (women) by another group (men). If we use an analogy to Marx's analysis of class conflict, we can say that males are like the bourgeoisie, or capitalists; they control most of the society's wealth, prestige, and power. Females are like the proletariat, or workers; they can acquire valuable resources only by following the dictates of their "bosses."

The Feminist Perspective: A significant component of the conflict approach to gender stratification draws on feminist theory. Feminist sociologists would find little to disagree with in the conflict theorists' perspective. But the feminist perspective would also argue that until recently, the very discussion of women and society, however well meant, was distorted by the exclusion of women from academic thought, including sociology.

The Interactionist View of Gender Stratification: While functionalists and conflict theorists who study gender stratification typically focus on macro-level social forces and institutions, interactionist researchers tend to examine gender stratification on the micro level of everyday behavior. For example, in conversations men are more likely than women to change the topic, to ignore topics chosen by members of the opposite sex, to minimize the contributions and ideas of members of the opposite sex, and to validate their own contributions. These patterns reflect the conversational (and, in a sense, political) dominance of males. From an interactionist perspective, these simple, day-to-day exchanges are one more battleground in the struggle for sexual equality—as women try to get a word in edgewise in the midst of men's interruptions and verbal dominance.

Women—The Oppressed Majority: When one looks at the political structure of the United States, women remain noticeably underrepresented. This lack of women in decision-making positions is evidence of women's powerlessness in the United States. Women can be said to suffer both from individual acts of sexism and from institutional sexism. All the major institutions of our society are controlled by men. These institutions, in their "normal" day-to-day operations, often discriminate against women and perpetuate sexism.

The Status of Women Worldwide: Women experience second-class treatment throughout the world. They constitute one-third of the world's paid labor force, but are generally found in the lowest-paying jobs. Single-parent households headed by women, which appear to be on the increase in many nations, are typically found in the poorest sections of the population. The feminization of poverty has become a global phenomenon.

Women in the Workforce of the United States: Women's participation in the paid labor force increased steadily throughout the twentieth century. A majority of women are now members of the paid labor force. Unfortunately, women entering the job market find their options restricted in important ways. Particularly damaging is occupational segregation, or confinement to sex-typed "women's jobs." Women from all groups and men from minority groups sometimes encounter attitudinal or organizational bias that prevents them from reaching their full potential. The **glass ceiling** refers to an invisible barrier that blocks the promotion of a qualified individual in a work environment.

Social Consequences of Women's Employment: Studies indicate that there is still a clear gender gap in the performance of housework, although it is narrowing. Women do more housework and spend more time on childcare than men do, whether on a workday or a non-workday. Sociologist Arlie Hochschild has used the phrase **second shift** to describe the double burden that many women face—work outside the home followed by child care and housework—and few men share equitably.

Aging and Society: "Being old" is a master status that commonly overshadows all others in the United States. Once people have been labeled "old," the designation has a major impact on how others perceive them, and even on how they view themselves. Negative stereotypes of the elderly contribute to their position as a minority group subject to discrimination. The elderly experience unequal treatment in employment, and may face prejudice and discrimination; they share physical characteristics that distinguish them from younger people; their membership in a disadvantaged minority is involuntary; they have a strong sense of group solidarity; and they are generally married to others of a comparable age.

Disengagement Theory: Elaine Cumming and William Henry introduced an explanation of the impact of aging during one's life course known as **disengagement theory**. This theory contends that society and the aging individual mutually sever many of their relationships. In keeping with the functionalist perspective, disengagement theory emphasizes that passing social roles on from one generation to another ensures social stability. Implicit in disengagement theory is the view that society should help older people to withdraw from their accustomed social roles. Although functionalist in its approach, disengagement theory ignores the fact that postretirement employment has been increasing in recent decades.

Activity Theory: Often seen as an opposing approach to disengagement theory, **activity theory** argues that the elderly person who remains active will be best adjusted. Proponents of activity theory view older people's withdrawal from society as harmful for both the elderly and society. Activity theorists focus on the potential contributions of older people to the maintenance of society. In their opinion, aging citizens will feel satisfied only when they can be useful and productive in society's terms, primarily by working for wages.

The Conflict Approach: Conflict theorists have criticized both disengagement theorists and activity theorists for failing to consider the impact of social structure on aging patterns. According to the conflict approach, the treatment of older people in the United States reflects the many divisions in our society. The low status of older people is seen in prejudice and discrimination against them, in age segregation, and in unfair job practices, none of which are directly addressed by either disengagement theory or activity theory.

Role Transitions throughout the Life Course: How we move through the life course varies dramatically, depending on the individual. Only in the most general terms, then, can we speak of stages or periods in the life course. The first transitional period marks the time at which an individual gradually enters the adult world. At about age 40, men and women often experience a stressful period of self-evaluation, commonly known as the **midlife crisis**. During the late 1990s, social scientists focused on the **sandwich generation**—adults who simultaneously try to meet the competing needs of their parents and their children.

Adjusting to Retirement: Retirement is a rite of passage that marks a critical transition from one phase of a person's life to another. Retirement is not a single transition, but rather a series of adjustments that varies from one person to another. Like other aspects of life in the United States, the experience of retirement varies according to gender, race, and ethnicity.

The "Graying of America": An increasing proportion of the population of the United States is composed of older people. Men and women aged 65 years and over constituted only 4.1 percent of the national population in the year 1900, but by 2010 this figure is expected to grow to 13 percent. In 2010, a higher percentage of non-Hispanic Whites are projected to be older than 65, compared to African Americans, Asian Americans, and Hispanics. These differences reflect the shorter life spans of the latter groups, as well as immigration patterns among Asians and Hispanics. Politicians court the votes of older people, since they are the age group most likely to register and vote.

The Battle over Abortion from a Global Perspective: A critical victory in the struggle for legalized abortion in the United States came in 1973, when the U.S. Supreme Court granted women the right to terminate pregnancies in the *Roe v. Wade* ruling. The debate that has followed *Roe v. Wade* revolves around prohibiting abortion altogether or, at the very least, putting limits on it. In 1979, for example, Missouri required parental consent for minors wishing to obtain an abortion, and the Supreme Court upheld the law. Sociologists see gender and social class as the defining issues surrounding abortion. In terms of social class, the first major restriction on the legal right to terminate a pregnancy affected poor people. In 1976, Congress passed the Hyde Amendment, which banned the use of Medicaid and other federal funds for abortions. Viewed from a conflict perspective, this is one more financial burden that falls especially heavily on low-income women.

KEY TERMS

Briefly define or identify the following terms in the spaces provided below. The definitions of these terms can be found later in this chapter of the study guide.

Gender role	Instrumentality
Homophobia	Expressiveness
Sexism	Institutional discrimination
Sexual harassment	Glass ceiling

Second shift	Feminism

SELF-TEST

MODIFIED TRUE/FALSE QUESTIONS: If the statement below is true, write "true" in the space provided. If the statement is false, briefly correct the error.

1. Azadeh Moaveni's research in Iran suggests that gender roles are fairly consistent from one society to another.

2. Gender roles are biologically determined.

3. The research of anthropologist Margaret Mead points to the importance of biological factors in defining the social roles of males and females.

4. Conflict theorists see gender differences as a reflection of the subjugation of one group (women) by another group (men).

5. By the year 2006, female representation in our political arenas was equal to that of men.

6. Among Muslims, both men and women are expected to cover themselves and avoid wearing revealing clothes in public.

7. In the U.S., women and men in the same occupations typically have very similar incomes.

8. Sociologist Michelle Budig found that men in predominantly female professions benefited from hidden advantages gained from their status as men.

9. Gerontologists rely heavily on sociological principles to explain the impact of aging on the individual and society.

10. According to activity theory, the approach of death forces people to drop most of their social roles, including those of worker, volunteer, spouse, hobby enthusiast, and even reader.

11. During the tragic 1995 heat wave that resulted in 733 deaths in Chicago, older Hispanics and Asian Americans had higher death rates from the heat wave than did other racial and ethnic groups.

12. Conflict theorists have criticized both disengagement theory and activity theory for failing to consider the impact of social structure on patterns of aging.

13. The term "sandwich generation" refers to older people who are providing support for their children and grandchildren simultaneously.

14.   NORCs are retirement communities established through a federal initiative, whose purpose is to create more communities for older people as the population ages.

15.   According to gerontologist Robert Atchley, the fourth stage of dying is depression.

MULTIPLE-CHOICE QUESTIONS: Read each question carefully and then select the best answer.

1.   The most crucial agent of socialization in teaching gender roles in the United States is
    a. peers.
    b. teachers.
    c. media personalities.
    d. parents.

2.   Which of the following statements is true?
    a. More boys than girls take AP exams.
    b. Women in the United States are more likely than men to attend college.
    c. Women in the U.S. are less likely than men to obtain doctoral degrees.
    d. all of the above

3.   Who discovered a culture in New Guinea where gender expectations were almost the reverse of those found in the United States?
        a. George Herbert Mead
        b. Robert Bales
        c. Margaret Mead
        d. Talcott Parsons

4.   Which sociological perspective makes a distinction between instrumental and expressive roles?

      a. the functionalist perspective

      b. the conflict perspective

      c. the interactionist perspective

      d. labeling theory

5.   Which sociological perspective emphasizes that the relationship between females and males has been one of unequal power, with men in a dominant position over women?

      a. the functionalist perspective

      b. the conflict perspective

      c. the interactionist perspective

      d. dramaturgical perspective

6.   Which sociological perspective acknowledges that it is not possible to change gender roles drastically without dramatic revisions in a culture's social structure?

      a. functionalist perspective

      b. conflict perspective

      c. interactionist perspective

      d. both a and b

7.   In studying gender stratification, which sociological perspective typically focuses on the micro level of everyday behavior, such as cross-sex conversation?

      a. the functionalist perspective

      b. the conflict perspective

      c. the interactionist perspective

      d. all of the above

8.   In 1981, Sandra Day O'Connor was sworn in as the nation's first female

      a. senator.

      b. governor.

      c. U.S. Supreme Court justice.

      d. attorney general.

9. In what way do female physicians interact differently with patients than do male physicians?
    a. They take on an aggressive interactional style to compensate for their lack of authority.
    b. They have poor bedside manner.
    c. They spend 10 percent more time with patients.
    d. both a and c

10. What are the two kinds of sexual harassment recognized by the courts?
    a. quid pro quo and a hostile environment.
    b. squid con so and a hostile environment.
    c. quid pro con and a hostile environment.
    d. none of the above

11. Which of the following statements about the status of women around the world is correct?
    a. They rarely own land.
    b. They generally work in the lowest-paid jobs.
    c. Households headed by single women are typically found in relatively poor areas.
    d. all of the above

12. In 2004, _____ percent of adult women in the United States held jobs outside the home.
    a. 24
    b. 38
    c. 59
    d. 87

13. Which sociologist has used the phrase second shift to describe the double burden—work outside the home followed by child care and housework—that many women face and few men share equitably?
    a. Heidi Hartmann
    b. Arlie Hochschild
    c. Talcott Parsons
    d. Kristin Luker

14. Which of the following statements about the elderly is correct?
    a. Being old is a master status.
    b. Once people are labeled as old, it has a major impact on how others perceive them.
    c. Once people are labeled as old, it has a major impact on how they view themselves.
    d. all of the above

15. What is the one crucial difference between older people and other subordinate groups, such as racial and ethnic minorities or women?
    a. Older people do not experience unequal treatment in employment.
    b. Older people have a strong sense of group solidarity and other groups do not.
    c. All of us who live long enough will eventually assume the ascribed status of being an older person.
    d. Older people are generally married to others of comparable age and other minorities do not marry within their group.

16. Which field of study was originally developed in the 1930s as an increasing number of social scientists became aware of the plight of the elderly?
    a. sociology
    b. gerontology
    c. gerontocracy
    d. senilicide

17. Elaine Cumming and William Henry introduced an explanation of the impact of aging known as
    a. disengagement theory.
    b. activity theory.
    c. labeling theory.
    d. the contact hypothesis.

18. Activity theory is associated with
    a. the functionalist perspective.
    b. the conflict perspective.
    c. the interactionist perspective.
    d. labeling theory.

19.   Which sociological perspective is most likely to emphasize the important role of social networks in providing life satisfaction for the elderly?
   a. the functionalist perspective
   b. the conflict perspective
   c. the interactionist perspective
   d. labeling theory

20.   Which sociological perspective views the treatment of older people as reflective of the many divisions in our society?
   a. functionalist perspective
   b. conflict perspective
   c. interactionist perspective
   d. labeling theory

21.   _____ theorists regard older people as victimized by social structure, with their social roles relatively unchanged but devalued.
   a. Functionalist
   b. Conflict
   c. Interactionist
   d. Dramaturgical

22.   Men and women often experience a stressful period of self-evaluation, commonly known as
   a. passage confusion.
   b. "old old" dementia.
   c. altimetry division.
   d. midlife crisis.

23.   Retirement is an example of a
   a. rite of passage.
   b. gerontocracy.
   c. functional prerequisite.
   d. trained incapacity.

24.   According to psychologist Elisabeth Kübler-Ross, the first stage of the experience
        of dying that a person may undergo is
        a. denial.
        b. anger.
        c. depression.
        d. bargaining.

25.   Which sociological perspective would be most likely to emphasize the tasks of
        those who are dying—for example, settling insurance and legacy matters,
        restoring harmony to social relationships, and making funeral plans?
        a. the functionalist perspective
        b. the conflict perspective
        c. the interactionist perspective
        d. labeling theory

FILL-IN QUESTIONS: Fill in the blank spaces in the sentences below with the correct
words. Where two or more words are required, there will be a corresponding number of
blank spaces.

1.   _____ contributes significantly to rigid gender-role socialization,
       since many people stereotypically associate male homosexuality with femininity
       and lesbianism with masculinity.

2.   Talcott Parsons and Robert Bales contend that women take the _____,
       emotionally supportive role in the family and that men take the
       _____, practical role.

3.   _____ theorists would say that males are like the bourgeoisie, or
       capitalists (they control most of society's wealth, prestige, and power) and that
       females are like the proletarians, or workers.

4.   Studies show that up to 96 percent of all interruptions in cross-sex (male-female)
       conversations are initiated by _____.

5.   It is not simply that particular men in the United States are biased in their
       treatment of women. All the major institutions of our society—including the
       government, armed forces, large corporations, the media, the universities, and the
       medical establishment—are controlled by men. This situation is symptomatic of
       institutional _____.

6.   Women from all groups and men from minority groups sometimes encounter attitudinal or organizational bias that prevents them from reaching their full potential. This is known as the _____ _____.

7.   Sociologist Arlie Hochschild has used the phrase _____ _____ to describe the double burden that many women face and few men share equitably: working outside the home followed by child care and housework.

8.   In keeping with the _____ perspective of sociology, disengagement theory emphasizes that a society's stability is ensured when social roles are passed on from one generation to another.

9.   The improved health of older people, which is sometimes overlooked by social scientists, has strengthened the arguments of _____ theorists regarding how society should deal with the elderly.

10.   _____ theorists argue that both the disengagement and the activity perspectives often ignore the impact of social class in the lives of the elderly.

11.   During the late 1990s, growing attention in the United States focused on the _____ generation: adults who simultaneously try to meet the competing needs of their parents and their children.

12.   According to Robert Atchley, the final phase of retirement is the _____ phase, which begins when the person can no longer engage in such basic, day-to-day activities as self-care and housework.

13.   _____ _____ programs provide treatment of the terminally ill in their own homes, or in special hospital units or other facilities, with the goal of helping them to die easily and without pain.

14.   The "old old" segment of the population of the United States—people _____ years old and over—is growing rapidly.

15.   A critical victory in the struggle for legalized abortion in the United States came in 1973 when the Supreme Court granted women the right to terminate pregnancies in the _____ v. _____ decision.

UNDERSTANDING SOCIAL POLICY: Each of the following questions is based on material that appears in the social policy section on "The Battle over Abortion from a Global Perspective." Write a brief answer to each question in the space provided below.

1.   What is at the heart of the abortion controversy in the United States today?

2.   In what way has changing technology had an impact on the abortion controversy?

3.   What is the sociological interest in abortion rights?

4.   In the battle between pro-choice and pro-life activists, what are the most recent policy initiatives that have been made with respect to abortion rights in the United States?

DEFINITIONS OF KEY TERMS

Gender role: Expectations regarding the proper behavior, attitudes, and activities of males and females.

Homophobia: Fear of and prejudice against homosexuality.

Instrumentality: An emphasis on tasks, a focus on more distant goals, and a concern for the external relationship between one's family and other social institutions.

Expressiveness: Concern for the maintenance of harmony and the internal emotional affairs of the family.

Sexism: The ideology that one sex is superior to the other.

Institutional discrimination: The denial of opportunities and equal rights to individuals and groups that results from the normal operations of a society.

Sexual harassment: Behavior that occurs when work benefits are made contingent on sexual favors (as a quid pro quo), or when touching, lewd comments, or the exhibition of pornographic material creates a "hostile environment" in the workplace.

Glass ceiling: An invisible barrier that blocks the promotion of a qualified individual in a work environment because of the individual's gender, race, or ethnicity.

Second shift: The double burden—work outside the home followed by child care and housework—that many women face and few men share equitably.

Feminism: The belief in social, economic, and political equality for women.

ANSWERS TO SELF-TEST

Modified True/False Questions

1. Moaveni found not only that gender roles are very different in Iran than they are in the United States, but also that they changed dramatically with the Iranian Revolution.

2. We socially construct our behavior so that male-female differences are either created or exaggerated.

3. The research of anthropologist Margaret Mead points to the importance of cultural conditioning—as opposed to biological factors—in defining the social roles of males and females.

4. True

5. Women remain noticeably underrepresented. In 2006, only 8 of the nation's 50 states had a female governor.

6. True

7. Data from the Census Bureau show that, even when women and men are in the same occupation, men typically earn more than women.

8. True

9. True

10. According to disengagement theory, the approach of death forces people to drop most of their social roles.

11. During the tragic 1995 heat wave that resulted in 733 deaths in Chicago, older Hispanics and Asian Americans had lower death rates from the heat wave than did other racial and ethnic groups.

12. True

13. The sandwich generation refers to adults who simultaneously try to meet the competing needs of their parents and their children.

14. NORCs are areas that have gradually become informal centers for senior citizens, not through any government initiative.

15. According to Elizabeth Kübler-Ross, the fourth stage of dying is depression.

Multiple-Choice Questions

1.	d	10.	a	19.	c
2.	b	11.	d	20.	b
3.	c	12.	c	21.	b
4.	a	13.	b	22.	d
5.	b	14.	d	23.	a
6.	d	15.	c	24.	a
7.	c	16.	b	25.	a
8.	c	17.	a		
9.	c	18.	c		

Fill-In Questions

1.	Homophobia	9.	activity
2.	expressive; instrumental	10.	Conflict
3.	Conflict	11.	sandwich
4.	men	12.	termination
5.	discrimination	13.	880,000
6.	glass ceiling	14.	Hospice care
7.	second shift	15.	*Roe, Wade*
8.	functionalist		

Understanding Social Policy: The Battle over Abortion from a Global Perspective

1.   A critical victory in the struggle for legalized abortion in the United States came in 1973 in the Supreme Court case of *Roe v. Wade*, which was based on a woman's right to privacy. The Court's decision was generally applauded by pro-choice groups, which believe that women should have the right to make their own decisions about their bodies and that they should have access to safe and legal abortions. However, for pro-life groups, abortion is a moral and often religious issue. In their view, human life begins at the moment of conception rather than at the moment of a baby's delivery, so that its termination through abortion is essentially an act of murder.

2.   "Day-after" pills are now prescribed in the United States. These pills can abort a fertilized egg the day after conception. Doctors, guided by ultrasound, can now end a pregnancy as early as eight days after conception. Pro-life activists are concerned that the use of ultrasound technology will allow people to abort unwanted females in nations where a premium is placed on male offspring.

3.   Sociologists see gender and social class as the defining issues surrounding abortion. The intense conflict over abortion reflects broader differences over women's position in society. Feminists involved in defending abortion rights typically believe that men and women are essentially similar; they support women's full participation in work outside the home and oppose all forms of sex discrimination. In contrast, most anti-abortion activists believe that men and women are fundamentally different. In their view, men are best suited to the public world of work, while women are best suited to the demanding and crucial task of rearing children. These activists are troubled by women's growing participation in work outside the home, which they view as destructive to the family, and ultimately to society.

4.   The Supreme Court currently supports the general right to terminate a pregnancy by a narrow 5-4 majority. While pro-life activists continue to hope for an overruling of *Roe v. Wade*, they have focused in the interim on weakening the decision through tactics such as limiting the use of fetal tissue in medical experiments and prohibiting late-term abortions. In 2005, speculation arose over a potential narrowing of the applicability of *Roe v. Wade* following the appointment of two new justices, John Roberts and Samuel Alito.

Global View of the Family

    Composition: What Is the Family?

    Kinship Patterns: To Whom Are We Related?

    Authority Patterns: Who Rules?

Studying the Family

    Functionalist View

    Conflict View

    Interactionist View

    Feminist View

Marriage and Family

    Courtship and Mate Selection

    Variations in Family Life and Intimate Relationships

    Child-Rearing Patterns in Family Life

Divorce

    Statistical Trends in Divorce

    Factors Associated with Divorce

    Impact of Divorce on Children

Diverse Lifestyles

    Cohabitation

    Remaining Single

    Marriage without Children

    Lesbian and Gay Relationships

Social Policy and the Family: Gay Marriage

    The Issue

    The Setting

    Sociological Insights

    Policy Initiatives

BOXES

    SOCIOLOGY IN THE GLOBAL COMMUNITY: *Domestic Violence*

    RESEARCH IN ACTION: *Arranged Marriage, American Style*

    RESEARCH IN ACTION: *The Lingering Impact of Divorce*

KEY POINTS

Composition—What Is a Family? A **family** can be defined as a set of people related by blood, marriage, some other agreed-upon relationship, or adoption, who share the primary responsibility for reproduction and caring for members of society. In the United States, many people still think of the family in very narrow terms—as a married couple and their unmarried children living together. However, this is but *one* type of family— what sociologists refer to as a **nuclear family**. By contrast, an **extended family** is a family in which relatives, in addition to parents and children, live in the same home.

Kinship Patterns—To Whom Are We Related? The state of being related to others is called **kinship**. The United States follows the system of **bilateral descent**, which means that both sides of a person's family are regarded as equally important. In **patrilineal descent,** only the father's relatives are important in terms of property, inheritance, and emotional ties. Conversely, in societies that favor **matrilineal descent**, only the mother's relatives are significant. New forms of reproductive technology will necessitate a new way of looking at kinship. Today, a combination of biological and social processes can "create" a family member, requiring that more distinctions be made about who is related to whom.

Authority Patterns—Who Rules? Societies vary in the way that power is distributed within the family. A society that expects males to dominate in all family decision making is termed a **patriarchy**. In contrast, in a **matriarchy**, women have greater authority than men. In a third type of authority pattern, the **egalitarian family**, spouses are regarded as equals. This does not mean, however, that all decisions are shared in such families. Wives may hold authority in some spheres, husbands in others.

Functionalist View of the Family: The family performs six paramount functions, first outlined more than 65 years ago by sociologist William F. Ogburn. These are (1) reproduction, (2) protection, (3) socialization, (4) regulation of sexual behavior, (5) affection and companionship, and (6) provision of social status.

Conflict View of the Family: Conflict theorists view the family not as a contributor to social stability, but as a reflection of the inequality in wealth and power that is found within the larger society. Feminist and conflict theorists note that the family has traditionally legitimized and perpetuated male dominance. While the egalitarian family has become a more common pattern in the United States in recent decades, male dominance within the family has hardly disappeared. Conflict theorists also view the family as an economic unit that contributes to societal injustice. Children inherit the privileged or less-than-privileged social and economic status of their parents.

Interactionist View: Interactionists focus on the micro level of family and other intimate relationships. They are interested in how individuals interact with one another, whether they are cohabiting partners or long-time married couples. Interactionists might, for example, study the relationship between parents and children in stepfamilies.

Feminist View: Feminist sociologists have taken a strong interest in the family as a social institution. Sociologists have looked particularly closely at how women's work outside the home impacts their child care and housework duties. Feminist theorists have urged social scientists and social agencies to rethink the notion that families in which no adult male is present are automatically cause for concern.

Parenthood: The socialization of children is essential to the maintenance of any culture. Consequently, parenthood is one of the most important (and most demanding) social roles in the United States. Sociologist Alice Rossi has identified four factors that complicate the transition to parenthood and the role of socializer. First, there is little anticipatory socialization for the social role of caregiver. Second, only limited learning occurs during the period of pregnancy itself. Third, the transition to parenthood is quite abrupt. Finally, in Rossi's view, our society lacks clear and helpful guidelines for successful parenthood. Recently, more adult children are living at home longer, or returning home after college. In 2004, 9 percent of all children lived in their grandparents homes.

Dual-Income Families: The idea of a family consisting of a wage-earning husband with a wife who stays at home has largely given way to the dual-income household. Among married people between the ages of 25 and 34, 95 percent of the men and 68 percent of the women were in the labor force in 2006. A major factor in the rise of dual-income couples is economic need. Other factors include the nation's declining birthrate, the increase in the proportion of women with a college education, the shift in the economy of the United States from manufacturing to service industries, and the impact of the feminist movement in changing women's consciousness.

Single-Parent Families: In 2004, a single parent headed about 20 percent of white families with children under 18, 29 percent of Hispanic families with children, and 59 percent of African American families with children. A family headed by a single mother faces especially difficult problems when the mother is a teenager. While 88 percent of single parents in the United States are mothers, the number of households headed by single fathers more than quadrupled over the period from 1980 to 2000.

Factors Associated with Divorce: Perhaps the most important factor in the increase in divorce in the last hundred years has been the greater social acceptance of divorce. More important, various religious denominations have relaxed their negative attitudes toward divorce, and most religious leaders no longer treat it as a sin. In addition, many states have adopted more liberal divorce laws, families are having fewer children, more couples can afford divorces, and increasing numbers of women are becoming less economically and emotionally dependent on their husbands.

Cohabitation: One of the most dramatic trends in recent years has been the tremendous increase in male-female couples who choose to live together without marrying, thereby engaging in what is commonly called **cohabitation**. The number of such households in the United States rose sixfold in the 1960s and increased another 72 percent between 1990 and 2000. Working couples are almost twice as likely to cohabit as college students, and half of all people involved in cohabitation in the United States have been previously married. In much of Europe, cohabitation is also very common. Government policies in these countries make few legal distinctions between married and unmarried couples or households.

Remaining Single: More and more people are postponing entry into first marriages. Over one out of every three households with children in the United States was a single-parent household. The trend toward maintaining a single lifestyle is related to the growing economic independence of young people. This trend is especially significant for women. Freed from financial needs, women don't necessarily need to marry to enjoy a satisfying life.

Gay Marriage: The idea of same-sex marriage strikes some people as only the latest of many attacks on traditional marriage. To others, it seems an overdue acknowledgment of the formal relationships that faithful, monogamous gay couples have long maintained. Functionalists have traditionally seen marriage as a social institution that is closely tied to human reproduction. But many same-sex couples are entrusted with the socialization of young children. Conflict theorists have charged that denial of the right to marry reinforces the second-class status of gays and lesbians. Interactionists generally avoid the policy question and focus instead on the nature of same-sex households.

KEY TERMS

Briefly define or identify the following terms in the spaces provided below. The definitions of these terms can be found later in this chapter of the study guide.

Family	Monogamy
Nuclear family	Serial monogamy
Extended family	Polygamy

Polygyny	Exogamy
Polyandry	Incest taboo
Kinship	Homogamy
Bilateral descent	Machismo
Patrilineal descent	Familism
Matrilineal descent	Adoption
Patriarchy	Single-parent family
Matriarchy	Cohabitation
Egalitarian family	Domestic partnership
Endogamy	

SELF-TEST

MODIFIED TRUE/FALSE QUESTIONS: If the statement below is true, write "true" in the space provided. If the statement is false, briefly correct the error.

1.   By 2000, more than one-half of all households in the United States fit the nuclear family model.

2.   In polygynous societies, most men have multiple spouses.

3.   Kinship is totally determined by biological or marital ties.

4.   Many sociologists believe that the matriarchal family has begun to replace the patriarchal family as the social norm in the United States, as more women become self-sufficient.

5.   The functionalist perspective encourages us to examine the ways in which the family gratifies the needs of its members and contributes to the stability of society.

6.   Currently, over 95 percent of all men and women in the United States marry at least once.

7.   Endogamy is intended to reinforce the cohesiveness of the group by suggesting to the young that they should marry someone "of our own kind."

8.   The number of interracial marriages between African Americans and Whites in the United States has increased more than seven times in recent decades, jumping from 51,000 in 1960 to 403,000 in 2006.

9.   Among the poor, adult women often play a significant role in the economic support of the family.

10.   Adopters must be married.

11.   Approximately 10 percent of all people in the United States will marry, divorce, and then remarry.

12.   Men are less likely to remarry than women are, because men cannot afford to make child support payments and establish a new family simultaneously.

13.   Cohabitation involves only male–female couples.

14.   The number of households in the United States engaged in cohabitation increased 72 percent between 1990 and 2000.

15.   Current data indicate that more people in the United States are entering marriage at an earlier age than was true in the past.

MULTIPLE-CHOICE QUESTIONS: Read each question carefully and then select the best answer.

1.   A family is defined in the text as
       a. a married couple and their unmarried children living together.

    b. an arrangement in which relatives such as grandparents, aunts, or uncles live in the same home as parents and their children.

    c. a set of people related by blood, marriage, some other agreed-upon relationship, or adoption, who share the primary responsibility for reproduction and caring for members of society.

    d. a group of friends who are referred to as members of a person's family.

2.   Alice, age 7, lives in a private home with her parents, her grandmother, and her aunt. Alice's family is an example of a(n) _____ family.

    a. nuclear

    b. dysfunctional

    c. extended

    d. polygynous

3.   The marriage of a woman to more than one man at the same time is referred to as

    a. polygny.

    b. monogamy.

    c. serial monogamy.

    d. polyandry.

4.   The form of marriage in which a person may have several spouses in his or her life but only one spouse at a time is referred to as

    a. serial monogamy.

    b. monogamy.

    c. polygamy.

    d. polyandry.

5.   According to anthropologist George Murdock, the most common type of polygamy is

    a. polygyny.

    b. polyandry.

    c. serial polygamy.

    d. matriarchy.

6.   Which system of descent is followed in the United States?

    a. matrilineal

    b. patrilineal

    c. unilateral

    d. bilateral

7.   In which type of society do women have greater authority than men?
        a.   matriarchal
        b.   patriarchal
        c.   egalitarian
        d.   authoritarian

8.   In the egalitarian authority pattern,
        a.   males are expected to dominate in all family decision making.
        b.   women have greater authority than men.
        c.   spouses are regarded as equals.
        d.   family mediators are generally consulted in matters of decision making.

9.   Which of the following is NOT a function of the family discussed by William Ogburn?
        a.   provision of social status
        b.   reproduction
        c.   economic support
        d.   protection

10.   Which sociological perspective views the family as a reflection of the inequality in wealth and power found within the larger society?
        a.   the functionalist perspective
        b.   the conflict perspective
        c.   the interactionist perspective
        d.   both b and c

11.   Which sociological perspective views the family as an economic unit that contributes to societal injustice?
        a.   the functionalist perspective
        b.   the conflict perspective
        c.   the interactionist perspective
        d.   both a and c

12.   Which of the following statements about male dominance in the family is true?
        a.   Egalitarian marriages are decreasing.
        b.   One in ten stay-at-home parents are stay-at-home dads, putting them at a power disadvantage in the home.
        c.   Some men maintain their dominance through acts of domestic violence.
        d.   Historically, laws and religion have promoted equality.

13.   In the United States in 2005, women earned more than their husbands in
        a. 16 percent of all couples.
        b. 26 percent of all couples.
        c. in 16 percent of couples that were divorcing.
        d. in 26 percent of couples that were divorcing.

14.   _____ focus on the micro level of the family, showing an interest, for
        example, in whether people are cohabiting partners or long-time married couples.
        a. Interactionists
        b. Functionalists
        c. Conflict theorists
        d. Systems theorists

15.   Which norm requires mate selection outside certain groups, usually one's own
        family or certain kinfolk?
        a. exogamy
        b. endogamy
        c. matriarchy
        d. patriarchy

16.   _____ is the conscious or unconscious tendency to select a mate with
        personal characteristics similar to one's own.
        a. Endogamy
        b. Exogamy
        c. Polygamy
        d. Homogamy

17.   Pride in the extended family among Mexican Americans is referred to as
        a. familism.
        b. machismo.
        c. bilateralism.
        d. extended family.

18.   One recent development in family life in the United States has been the extension
        of parenthood as adult children continue to (or return to) live at home. The reason
        for this is
        a. the rising divorce rate.
        b. skyrocketing rent and real estate prices.

    c.   financial difficulties.

    d.   all of the above

19.   What term has been used in the popular press to refer to adult children who continue to (or return to) live at home?

    a.   the "boomerang generation"

    b.   counterculture

    c.   the "Brady Bunch" cohort

    d.   Generation X

20.   Which sociological perspective emphasizes that government has a strong interest in encouraging adoption?

    a.   the functionalist perspective

    b.   the conflict perspective

    c.   the interactionist perspective

    d.   labeling theory

21.   Which of the following is a factor that has contributed to the rise of the dual-income model of the family?

    a.   increasing number of men with a college education

    b.   increasing birthrate

    c.   shift in the economy of the United States from manufacturing to service industries

    d.   all of the above

22.   Since 1980, the rate of teenage pregnancy among African Americans in the United States has

    a.   increased dramatically.

    b.   decreased.

    c.   increased slightly.

    d.   remained steady.

23.   Of those in the United States who obtain a divorce, about _____ percent later remarry.

    a.   10

b. 45

c. 63

d. 80

24. Which of the following factors is associated with the high divorce rate in the United States?
      a. the liberalization of divorce laws
      b. contemporary families having fewer children than earlier families
      c. the increase in family incomes
      d. all of the above

25. In 1999, _____ gave gay couples the legal benefits of marriage through civil union; then, in 2003, the _____ Supreme Court ruled that under the state's constitution, gay couples have the right to marry.
      a. Minnesota; New York
      b. Vermont; Massachusetts
      c. New York; California
      d. Oregon; Hawaii

FILL-IN QUESTIONS: Fill in the blank spaces in the sentences below with the correct words. Where two or more words are required, there will be a corresponding number of blank spaces.

1. People in the United States see the _____ family as the preferred form of family arrangement.

2. Anthropologist George Murdock sampled 565 societies and found that over 80 percent had some type of _____ as their preferred form of marriage.

3. The principle of _____ assigns people to kinship groups according to their relationship to an individual's mother or father.

4. In patriarchal societies, the _____ male often wields the greatest power.

5.   _____ emerged among Native American tribal societies, and in nations in which men were absent for long periods for warfare or food gathering.

6.   In the view of many sociologists, the _____ family has begun to replace the patriarchal family as the social norm in the United States.

7.   As _____ theorists point out, the social class of parents significantly influences children's socialization experiences and the degree of protection they receive.

8.   Mate selection based on love is not a cultural universal. In many societies, marriages are instead _____ by parents or religious authorities.

9.   Although social class differences in family life are less striking than they once were, _____ class families were found to be more authoritarian in rearing children and more inclined to use physical punishment.

10.   Caring for children is a(n) _____ function of the family, yet the ways in which different societies assign this function to family members can vary significantly.

11.   Sociologist Alice Rossi points out that there is little _____ socialization in the United States for the social roles of caregiver.

12.   Viewed from a(n) _____ perspective, having a child may provide a sense of motivation and purpose for a low-income teenager whose economic worth in our society is limited at best.

13.   Although _____ percent of single parents in the United States are mothers, the number of households headed by single fathers has more than _____ over the period from 1980 to 2000.

14.   The rising rates of divorce and remarriage in the United States have led to a noticeable increase in _____ relationships.

15.   Certain municipalities have passed legislation allowing for the registration of _____ _____, couples who live in close and committed personal relationships, but have not married.

UNDERSTANDING SOCIAL POLICY: Each of the following questions is based on material that appears in the social policy section on "Gay Marriage." Write a brief answer to each question in the space provided below.

1.   How do functionalists, conflict theorists, and interactionists view gay marriage?

2.   Describe recent policy changes toward gay marriage and civil unions.

3.   Describe public opinion toward gay marriage and civil unions.

DEFINITIONS OF KEY TERMS

Family: A set of people related by blood, marriage or some other agreed-upon relationship, or adoption, who share the primary responsibility for reproducing and caring for members of society.

Nuclear family: A married couple and their unmarried children living together.

Extended family: A family in which relatives—such as grandparents, aunts, or uncles—live in the same home as parents and their children.

Monogamy: A form of marriage in which one woman and one man are married only to each other.

Serial monogamy: A form of marriage in which a person may have several spouses in his or her lifetime, but only one spouse at a time.

Polygamy: A form of marriage in which an individual may have several husbands or wives simultaneously.

Polygyny: A form of polygamy in which a man may have more than one wife at the same time.

Polyandry: A form of polygamy in which a woman may have more than one husband at the same time.

Kinship: The state of being related to others.

Bilateral descent: A kinship system in which both sides of a person's family are regarded as equally important.

Patrilineal descent: A kinship system in which only the father's relatives are significant.

Matrilineal descent: A kinship system in which only the mother's relatives are significant.

Patriarchy: A society in which men dominate in family decision making.

Matriarchy: A society in which women dominate in family decision making.

Egalitarian family: An authority pattern in which spouses are regarded as equals.

Endogamy: The restriction of mate selection to people within the same group.

Exogamy: The requirement that people select a mate outside certain groups.

Incest taboo: The prohibition of sexual relationships between certain culturally specified relatives.

Homogamy: The conscious or unconscious tendency to select a mate with personal characteristics similar to one's own.

Machismo: A sense of virility, personal worth, and pride in one's maleness.

Familism: Pride in the extended family, expressed through the maintenance of close ties and strong obligations to kinfolk outside the immediate family.

Adoption: In a legal sense, a process that allows for the transfer of the legal rights, responsibilities, and privileges of parenthood to a new legal parent or parents.

Single-parent family: A family in which only one parent is present to care for the children.

Cohabitation: The practice of living together as a male-female couple without marrying.

Domestic partnership: Two unrelated adults who share a mutually caring relationship, reside together, and agree to be jointly responsible for their dependents, basic living expenses, and other common necessities.

ANSWERS TO SELF-TEST

Modified True/False Questions

1. By 2000 only about one-third of the nation's families fit the nuclear family model.

2. In polygynous societies, relatively few men actually have multiple spouses.

3. Kinship is culturally learned and is not totally determined by biological or marital ties.

4. Many sociologists believe the egalitarian family has begun to replace the patriarchal family as the social norm in the United States.

5. True

6. True

7. True

8. True

9. True

10. In some cases, adopters are not married and are not required to be married.

11. Approximately 45 percent of all people in the United States will marry, divorce, and then remarry.

12. Women are less likely to remarry than men are, because women most often retain custody of children after a divorce, which complicates establishing a new adult relationship.

13. True

14. True

15. Current data indicate that more people in the United States are postponing entry into first marriages than was true in the past.

Multiple-Choice Questions

1. c	10. b	19. a
2. c	11. b	20. a
3. d	12. c	21. c
4. a	13. b	22. b
5. a	14. a	23. c
6. d	15. a	24. d
7. a	16. d	25. b
8. c	17. a	
9. c	18. d	

Fill-In Questions

1. nuclear	9. lower
2. polygamy	10. universal
3. descent	11. anticipatory
4. eldest	12. interactionist
5. Matriarchies	13. 82; quadrupled
6. egalitarian	14. stepfamily
7. conflict	15. domestic partners
8. arranged	

Understanding Social Policy: Gay Marriage

1. Functionalists have traditionally seen marriage as a social institution that is closely tied to human reproduction. Many same-sex couples are entrusted with the socialization of young children, whether or not their partnership is recognized by the state. Conflict theorists have charged that the denial of the right to marry reinforces the second-class status of gays and lesbians. Interactionists generally avoid the policy questions and focus instead on the nature of same-sex households.

2. In 1999, Vermont gave gay couples the legal benefits of marriage through civil union. Then, in 2003, the Massachusetts Supreme Court ruled 4-3 that under the state's constitution, gay couples have the right to marry—a ruling the U.S. Supreme Court has refused to review. Many local jurisdictions have also passed legislation allowing for the registration of domestic partnerships, and have extended employees benefits to those relationships. Recently, pressure has been mounting for national legislation. The Defense of Marriage Act, passed in 1996, provided that no state is obliged to recognize same-sex marriages performed in another state. In 2003, opponents of gay marriage proposed a constitutional amendment that would limit marriage to heterosexual couples.

3. Recently, national surveys of attitudes toward gay marriage have been showing volatile shifts in public opinion. Typically, people are more opposed to gay marriage than to civil union: about one-fourth of respondents favor gay marriage, while as many as half favor civil union. Still, as of 2005, the majority of the population endorsed a constitutional amendment to ban gay marriage.

CHAPTER

13 EDUCATION AND RELIGION

Sociological Perspectives on Education
- Functionalist View
- Conflict View
- Feminist View
- Interactionist View

Schools as Formal Organizations
- Bureaucratization of Schools
- Teachers: Employees and Instructors
- Student Subcultures
- Homeschooling

Durkheim and the Sociological Approach to Religion

World Religions

Sociological Perspective on Religion
- Religion and Social Support
- Religion and Social Change
- Religion and Social Control: A Conflict View
- Feminist Perspective

Components of Religion
- Belief
- Ritual
- Experience

Religious Organization
- Ecclesiae
- Denominations
- Sects
- New Religious Movements or Cults
- Comparing Forms of Religious Organization

Case Study: Religion in India
- The Religious Tapestry in India
- Religion and the State in India

Social Policy and Religion: Religion in the Schools
- The Issue
- The Setting
- Sociological Insights
- Policy Initiatives

BOXES
- **TAKING SOCIOLOGY TO WORK:** Ray Zapata, Business Owner and Former Regent, Texas State University
- **SOCIOLOGY ON CAMPUS:** The Debate over Title IX
- **PHOTO ESSAY:** Why Do Sociologists Study Religion
- **RESEARCH IN ACTION:** Income and Education, Religiously Speaking
- **RESEARCH IN ACTION:** Islam in the United States

KEY POINTS

Transmitting Culture: As a social institution, education performs a rather conservative function: transmitting the dominant culture. Schooling exposes each generation of young people to the existing beliefs, norms, and values of their culture. In our society, we learn respect for social control and reverence for established institutions such as religion, the family, and the presidency.

Promoting Social and Political Integration: Education serves the latent function of promoting social and political integration by transforming a population composed of diverse racial, ethnic, and religious groups into a society whose members share—to some extent—a common identity. From a functionalist perspective, the common identity and social integration fostered by education contribute to societal stability and consensus. In the past, the integrative function of education was most obvious in its emphasis on promoting a common language.

Maintaining Social Control: Through the exercise of social control, schools teach students various skills and values essential to their future positions in the labor force. Schools direct and even restrict students' aspirations in a manner that reflects societal values and prejudices. Socialization into traditional gender roles can be viewed as a form of social control.

Conflict View of Schooling: The functionalist perspective portrays contemporary education as a basically benign institution. For example, it argues that schools rationally sort and select students for future high-status positions, thereby meeting society's need for talented and expert personnel. In contrast, the conflict perspective views education as an instrument of elite domination. Conflict theorists point out the sharp inequalities that exist in the educational opportunities available to different racial and ethnic groups.

Bestowal of Status: Conflict sociologists stress that schools sort pupils according to social class background. Although the educational system helps certain poor children to move into middle-class professional positions, it denies most disadvantaged children the same educational opportunities afforded to children of the affluent. In this way, schools tend to preserve social class inequalities in each new generation. Even a single school can reinforce class differences by putting students in tracks. Thus, working-class children, assumed to be destined for subordinate positions, are likely to be placed in high school vocational and general tracks, which emphasize close supervision and compliance with authority.

Treatment of Women in Education: In the twentieth century, sexism in education showed up in many ways—in textbooks with negative stereotypes of women, counselors' pressure on female students to prepare for "women's work," and unequal funding for women's and men's athletic programs. But perhaps nowhere was educational discrimination more evident than in the employment of teachers. Men generally filled the positions of university professor and college administrator, which hold relatively high status in the United States.

Education—The Interactionist View: The labeling approach suggests that if we treat people in particular ways, they may fulfill our expectations. A dominant group's stereotyping of racial minorities may limit their opportunities to break away from expected roles. Studies in the United States have revealed that teachers wait longer for an answer from a student they believe to be a high achiever, and they are more likely to give such children a second chance.

Schools as Formal Organizations: Max Weber noted five basic characteristics of bureaucracy, all of which are evident in the vast majority of schools. (1) A division of labor: Specialized experts teach particular age levels and specific subjects. (2) Hierarchy of authority: Each employee of a school system is responsible to a higher authority. (3) Written rules and regulations: Teachers and administrators must conform to numerous rules and regulations in the performance of their duties. (4) Impersonality: Large class sizes and bureaucratic norms encourage teachers to treat all students in the same way. (5) Employment based on technical qualifications: At least in theory, the hiring of instructors is based on professional competence and expertise.

Émile Durkheim: Émile Durkheim was perhaps the first sociologist to recognize the critical importance of religion in human societies. He saw its appeal for the individual, but more importantly, he stressed the social impact of religion. In Durkheim's view, religion is a collective act that includes many forms of behavior in which people interact with others. Durkheim defined **religion** as a "unified system of beliefs and practices relative to sacred things."

The Integrative Function of Religion: Émile Durkheim viewed religion as an integrative power in human society, a perspective that is reflected in functionalist thought today. Religion gives people certain ultimate values and ends to hold in common. In some instances, however, religious loyalties are dysfunctional; that is, they contribute to tension and even conflict between groups or nations.

Religion and Social Support: Through its emphasis on the divine and supernatural, religion allows us to "do something" about the calamities we face. Religion encourages us to view our personal misfortunes as relatively unimportant in the broader perspective of human history, or even as part of an undisclosed divine purpose. This perspective may be much more comforting than the terrifying feeling that any of us can die senselessly at any moment, and that there is no divine answer as to why one person lives a long and full life, whereas another dies tragically at a relatively early age.

Religion and Social Change—The Weberian Thesis: Max Weber carefully examined the connection between religious allegiance and capitalist development in his pioneering work *The Protestant Ethic and the Spirit of Capitalism*. Weber pointed out that the followers of John Calvin, a leader of the Protestant Reformation, emphasized a disciplined work ethic, this-worldly concerns, and a rational orientation to life that has become known as the **Protestant ethic**. Like Durkheim, Weber demonstrated that religion is not solely a matter of intimate personal beliefs. He stressed that the collective nature of religion has social consequences for society as a whole.

Religion and Social Change—A Conflict View: For Karl Marx, the relationship between religion and social change was clear: Religion impeded social change by encouraging oppressed people to focus on otherworldly concerns rather than on their immediate poverty or exploitation. He felt that religion often drugged the masses into submission by offering a consolation for their harsh lives on earth: the hope of salvation in an ideal afterlife. Marxists suggest that by inducing a "false consciousness" among the disadvantaged, religion lessens the possibility of collective political action that can end capitalist oppression and transform society.

Feminist Perspective: Women play a fundamental role in the religious socialization of children. However, most faiths have a long tradition of exclusively male leadership. Religion serves to subordinate women. Women make up 51percent of the students enrolled in theological schools, but account for only 12.8 percent of the clergy. They tend to have shorter careers, and to serve outside of congregational leadership.

Components of Religion: Religious beliefs, religious rituals, and religious experience all help to define what is sacred, and to differentiate the sacred from the profane. **Religious beliefs** are statements to which members of a particular religion adhere. **Religious rituals** are practices required or expected of members of a faith. The term **religious experience** refers to the feeling or perception of being in direct contact with the ultimate reality, such as a divine being, or of being overcome with religious emotion.

Religious Organization: Sociologists find it useful to distinguish among four basic forms of religious organization. An **ecclesia** is a religious organization that claims to include most or all members of a society, and is recognized as the national or official religion. A **denomination** is a large, organized religion that is not officially linked with the state or government. A **sect** can be defined as a relatively small religious group that has broken away from some other religious organization to renew what it considers the original vision of the faith. A **new religious movement** or **cult** is generally a small, secretive religious group that represents either a new religion or a major innovation of an existing faith.

Religion in India—A Case Study: Hinduism and Islam are the two most important religions in India. Today, Muslims account for 12 percent of India's population; Hindus make up 74 percent. Another religion, the Sikh faith, originated in the fifteenth century A.D. Sikhism shows the influence of Islam in India, in that it is monotheistic. A fourth faith that has been influential beyond its numbers in India is Jainism. According to the

Jain faith, there is no god; each person is responsible for his or her own spiritual well-being. Religion was influential in India's drive to overturn British colonialism. A proponent of nonviolent resistance, Gandhi persuaded Hindus and Muslims, ancient enemies, to join in defying British domination.

Religion in the Schools: The government must protect the right to practice one's religion; on the other hand, it cannot take any measures that would seem to "establish" one religion over another (the separation of church and state). In the key case of *Engle v. Vitale*, the U.S. Supreme Court ruled in 1962 that the use of nondenominational prayer in New York schools was "wholly inconsistent" with the First Amendment's prohibition against government establishment of religion. In the "monkey trial" of 1925, a high school biology teacher, John T. Scopes, was convicted of violating a Tennessee law making it a crime to teach the scientific theory of evolution in schools. Drawing on the interactionist perspective and small-group research, opponents of school prayer and creationism suggest that children will face enormous social pressure to conform to the beliefs and practices of a religious majority.

KEY TERMS

Briefly define or identify the following terms in the spaces provided below. The definitions of these terms can be found later in this chapter of the study guide.

Cultural universal	Liberation theology
Secularization	Religious belief
Education	Religious ritual
Religion	Religious experience
Sacred	Ecclesia
Profane	Denomination

Protestant ethic	Sect
Established Sect	Correspondence principle
New Religious Movement (NRM) or Cult	Teacher-expectancy effect
Hidden curriculum	Creationism
Credentialism	Intelligent design
Tracking	

SELF-TEST

MODIFIED TRUE/FALSE QUESTIONS: If the statement below is true, write "true" in the space provided. If the statement is false, briefly correct the error.

1.   Through the exercise of social control, schools teach students various skills and values essential to their future positions within the labor force. They learn punctuality, discipline, scheduling, and responsible work habits, as well as how to negotiate their way through the complexities of a bureaucratic organization.

2.   As early as 1916, Karl Marx had already anticipated the phenomenon of credentialism.

3.   It has been estimated that in the United States, about 2 percent of elementary schools and 3 percent of secondary schools use some form of tracking.

4. The labeling approach suggests that if we treat people in a particular way, they may fulfill our expectations.

5. Female participation in high school sports has doubled since Title IX was implemented.

6. Teachers are employees of formal organizations with bureaucratic structure.

7. The same object can be either sacred or profane, depending on how it is viewed.

8. A church service is a meeting ground for unmarried members. This is a manifest function of religions.

9. In Max Weber's *The Protestant Ethic and the Spirit of Capitalism*, he noted that in European nations with both Jewish and Protestant citizens, an overwhelming number of business leaders, owners of capital, and skilled workers were Jewish.

10. Karl Marx argued that religion impeded social change by encouraging oppressed people to focus on otherworldly concerns rather than on their immediate poverty or exploitation.

11. In the modern world, ecclesiae tend to be increasing in power.

12.   Denominations resemble sects in that generally few demands are made on members.

13.   Because of its immigrant heritage, the United States is home to a large number of denominations.

14.   Different Muslim sects are sometimes antagonistic toward each other.

15.   Although Hindus and Muslims joined together to defy British colonization, immediately after independence India was divided into two separate states: Pakistan for the Muslims and India for the Hindus.

MULTIPLE-CHOICE QUESTIONS: Read each question carefully and then select the best answer.

1.   The most basic manifest function of education is
        a. transmitting culture.
        b. transmitting knowledge.
        c. serving as an agent of change.
        d. maintaining social control.

2.   In 1996, Great Britain's chief curriculum adviser proposed that British schools socialize students into a set of core values that included
        a. a sense of fair play.
        b. politeness.
        c. faithfulness.
        d. all of the above

3.   Which of the following was introduced into school systems to promote social change?

   a.   sex education classes
   b.   affirmative action programs
   c.   Project Head Start
   d.   all of the above

4.   Who coined the term "hidden curriculum" to refer to standards of behavior that are deemed proper by society and are taught subtly in schools?

   a.   Max Weber
   b   Philip Jackson
   c.   Christopher Hurn
   d.   Émile Durkheim

5.   The trend toward credentialism was anticipated as far back as 1916 by

   a.   Émile Durkheim.
   b.   Max Weber.
   c.   Karl Marx.
   d.   Charles Horton Cooley.

6.   Which sociological perspective emphasizes that the widening bestowal of status granted by the educational system is beneficial not only to particular recipients but to the society as a whole?

   a.   the functionalist perspective
   b.   the conflict perspective
   c.   the interactionist perspective
   d.   labeling approach

7.   Which perspective contends that schools tend to preserve social class inequalities in each new generation?

   a.   the functionalist perspective
   b.   the conflict perspective
   c.   the interactionist perspective
   d.   anomie theory

8.   The correspondence principle was developed by
        a. Max Weber.
        b. Karl Marx and Friedrich Engels.
        c. Samuel Bowles and Herbert Gintis.
        d. James Thurber.

9.   The teacher-expectancy effect is most closely associated with
        a. the functionalist perspective.
        b. the conflict perspective.
        c. the interactionist perspective.
        d. anomie theory.

10.   Which of the following is NOT required by Title IX legislation?
        a. Require all-male athletic teams to accept women.
        b. Eliminate sex-segregated classes.
        c. Provide more opportunities for women to play sports.
        d. End sex discrimination in admissions and financial aid.

11.   The student subculture that is hostile to the college environment and seeks out ideas that may or may not relate to studies is called the
        a. collegiate subculture.
        b. academic subculture.
        c. vocational subculture.
        d. nonconformist subculture.

12   Which of the following sociologists stressed the social impact of religion, and was perhaps the first to recognize the critical importance of religion in human societies?
        a. Max Weber
        b. Émile Durkheim
        c. Karl Marx
        d. Talcott Parsons

13.   Religion defines the spiritual world and gives meaning to the divine. These are _____ functions of religion.
        a. manifest
        b. latent
        c. positive
        d. negative

14. Which sociological perspective emphasizes the integrative power of religion in human society?
    a. the functionalist perspective
    b. the conflict perspective
    c. the interactionist perspective
    d. all of the above

15. A Roman Catholic parish church offers services in the native language of an immigrant community. This is an example of
    a. the integrative function of religion.
    b. the social support function of religion.
    c. the social control function of religion.
    d. none of the above

16. John Calvin, a leader of the Protestant Reformation, emphasized
    a. a disciplined work ethic.
    b. this-worldly concerns.
    c. a rational orientation to life.
    d. all of the above

17. In Max Weber's pioneering work *The Protestant Ethic and the Spirit of Capitalism*, one by-product of Protestantism was
    a. a drive to accumulate savings.
    b. a commitment to serve God without pursuit of tangible items.
    c. a recognition that "God's will" will be understood another time.
    d. none of the above

18. Liberation theology is the use of the Roman Catholic church in a political effort to eliminate poverty, discrimination, and other forms of injustice, especially in
    a. Europe.
    b. East Africa.
    c. Latin America.
    d. Southeast Asia.

19.   Which sociological perspective argues that to whatever extent religion actually does influence social behavior, it reinforces existing patterns of dominance and inequality?

    a.   the functionalist perspective

    b.   the conflict perspective

    c.   the interactionist perspective

    d.   all of the above

20.   The Adam and Eve account of creation found in Genesis, the first book of the Old Testament, is an example of a religious

    a.   ritual.

    b.   experience.

    c.   custom.

    d.   belief.

21.   Which one of the following religious denominations is most likely to report the experience of being "born again"?

    a.   Southern Baptists

    b.   Roman Catholics

    c.   Episcopalians

    d.   Unitarians

22.   Which of the following is NOT an example of an ecclesia?

    a.   the Lutheran church in Sweden

    b.   Islam in Saudi Arabia

    c.   Buddhism in Thailand

    d.   the Episcopal church in the United States

23.   In a society with a(n) _____, the political and religious institutions often act in harmony and mutually reinforce each other's powers over their relative spheres of influence.

    a.   denomination

    b.   ecclesia

    c.   cult

    d.   sect

24.   By far the largest single denomination in the United States is
   a. Lutheranism.
   b. Episcopalianism.
   c. Southern Baptists.
   d. Roman Catholicism.

25.   Which of the following has a set of doctrines that are innovative and
pathbreaking?
   a. cults
   b. ecclesiae
   c. denominations
   d. sects

FILL-IN QUESTIONS: Fill in the blank spaces in the sentences below with the correct words. Where two or more words are required, there will be a corresponding number of blank spaces.

1.   From a(n) _____ perspective, the common identity and social integration fostered by education contributes to societal stability and consensus.

2.   In the past, the integrative function of education was most obvious through its emphasis on promoting a common _____.

3.   _____ _____ in admissions—giving priority to females or minorities—has been endorsed as a means of countering racial and sexual discrimination.

4.   Numerous sociological studies have revealed that _____ years of formal schooling are associated with openness to new ideas and more _____ social and political viewpoints.

5.   _____ theorists have observed that credentialism may reinforce social inequality and may be especially damaging for applicants from poor and minority backgrounds.

6.   In the twentieth century, _____ in education has been manifested in many ways: in textbooks with negative stereotypes of women, in counselors' pressure on female students to prepare for "women's work," and in unequal funding for women's and men's athletic programs.

7. The bureaucratic characteristic of written rules and regulations can become _____ in schools, since the time invested in completing required forms could instead be spent in preparing lessons or conferring with students.

8. _____ _____ noted that in European nations with both Protestant and Catholic citizens, an overwhelming number of business leaders, owners of capital, and skilled workers were Protestant.

9. _____ theorists caution that Weber's theory of the Protestant ethic, even if it is accepted, should not be regarded as an analysis of mature capitalism as reflected in the rise of large corporations that transcend national boundaries.

10. In _____ _____ view, religion impeded social change by encouraging oppressed people to focus on other-worldly concerns rather than on their immediate poverty or exploitation.

11. _____ _____ are statements to which members of a particular religion adhere.

12. The single largest denomination in the United States is _____ _____.

13. Unlike ecclesiae and denominations, _____ require intensive commitments and demonstrations of belief by members.

14. Seventy-four percent of India's population practice _____.

15. The "big bang" theory is challenged by _____ who hold to the biblical account of the creation of humans and the universe.

UNDERSTANDING SOCIAL POLICY: All of the following questions are based on material that appears in the social policy section on Religion in the Schools. Write a brief answer to each question in the space provided below.

1. What is creationism and why is it a social issue in the United States?

2. What was the "monkey trial"?

3.   What do opponents of school prayer and creationism argue?

DEFINITIONS OF KEY TERMS

Cultural universal: A common practice or belief found in every culture.

Secularization: The process through which religion's influence on other social institutions diminishes.

Education: A formal process of learning in which some people consciously teach while others adopt the social role of learner.

Religion: A unified system of beliefs and practices relative to sacred things.

Sacred: Elements beyond everyday life that inspire awe, respect, and even fear.

Profane: The ordinary and commonplace elements of life, as distinguished from the sacred.

Protestant ethic: Max Weber's term for the disciplined work ethic, this-worldly concerns, and rational orientation to life emphasized by John Calvin and his followers.

Liberation theology: Use of a church, primarily Roman Catholicism, in a political effort to eliminate poverty, discrimination, and other forms of injustice from a secular society.

Religious belief: A statement to which members of a particular religion adhere.

Religious ritual: A practice required or expected of members of a faith.

Religious experience: The feeling or perception of being in direct contact with the ultimate reality, such as a divine being, or of being overcome with religious emotion.

Ecclesia: A religious organization that claims to include most or all members of a society and is recognized as the national or official religion.

Denomination: A large, organized religion that is not officially linked to the state or government.

Sect: A relatively small religious group that has broken away from some other religious organization to renew what it considers the original vision of the faith.

Established sect: A religious group that is the outgrowth of a sect, yet remains isolated from society.

New Religious Movement (NRM) or **cult**: A small, secretive religious group that represents either a new religion or a major innovation of an existing faith.

Hidden curriculum: Standards of behavior that are deemed proper by society and are taught subtly in schools.

Credentialism: An increase in the lowest level of education required to enter a field.

Tracking: The practice of placing students in specific curriculum groups on the basis of test scores and other criteria.

Correspondence principle: The tendency of schools to promote the values expected of individuals in each social class and to prepare students for the types of jobs typically held by members of their class.

Teacher-expectancy effect: The impact that a teacher's expectations about a student's performance may have on the student's actual achievements.

Creationism: A literal interpretation of the Bible regarding the creation of humanity and the universe, used to argue that evolution should not be presented as established scientific fact.

Intelligent design: The idea that life is so complex, it could only have been created by intelligent design.

ANSWERS TO SELF-TEST

Modified True/False Questions

1. True

2. As early as 1916, Max Weber had already anticipated the phenomenon of credentialism.

3. It has been estimated that in the United States, about 60 percent of elementary schools and 80 percent of secondary schools use some form of tracking.

4. True

5. In 1971—just before Title IX was implemented—only 300,000 girls participated in high school sports. In 2003, the figure was 2.7 million.

6. True

7. True

8. Church services are a meeting ground for unmarried members. This is a latent function of religions.

9. In Max Weber's *The Protestant Ethic and the Spirit of Capitalism*, he noted that in European nations with both Catholic and Protestant citizens, an overwhelming number of business leaders, owners of capital, and skilled workers were Protestants.

10. True

11. In the modern world, ecclesiae tend to be declining in power.

12. Denominations resemble ecclesiae in that generally few demands are made on members.

13. True

14. True

15. True

Multiple-Choice Questions

1. b	10. a	19. b
2. d	11. d	20. d
3. d	12. b	21. a
4. b	13. a	22. d
5. b	14. a	23. b
6. a	15. a	24. d
7. b	16. d	25. a
8. c	17. a	
9. c	18. c	

Fill-In Questions

1. functionalist
2. language
3. Affirmative action
4. increased; liberal
5. Conflict
6. sexism
7. dysfunctional
8. Max Weber
9. Conflict
10. Karl Marx's
11. Religious beliefs
12. Roman Catholicism
13. sects
14. Hinduism
15. creationists

Understanding Social Policy: Religion in the Schools

1. Creationism is a literal interpretation of the Bible regarding the creation of humanity and the universe, used to argue that evolution should not be presented as established scientific fact. Creationists want their theory taught in schools as the only theory, or at the very least, as an alternative to the theory of evolution.

2. The controversy over whether the biblical account of creation should be presented in schools recalls the famous "monkey trial" of 1925. In that trial, high school biology teacher John T. Scopes was convicted of violating a Tennessee law making it a crime to teach the scientific theory of evolution in public schools.

3. Opponents of school prayer and creationism argue that a religious majority in a community might impose religious viewpoints specific to its faith, at the expense of religious minorities.

CHAPTER

14 GOVERNMENT AND THE ECONOMY

Economic Systems
 Capitalism
 Socialism
 The Informal Economy

Case Study: Capitalism in China
 The Road to Capitalism
 The Chinese Economy Today
 *Chinese Workers in the New
  Economy*

Power and Authority
 Power
 Types of Authority

Types of Government
 Monarchy
 Oligarchy
 Dictatorship and Totalitarianism
 Democracy

Political Behavior in the United States
 Participation and Apathy
 Race and Gender in Politics

*Models of Power Structure in the
United States*
 Power Elite Models
 Pluralist Model

War and Peace
 War
 Peace
 Terrorism

Changing Economies
 Microfinancing
 The Changing Face of the Workforce
 Deindustrialization

*Social Policy and the Economy: Global
Offshoring*
 The Issue
 The Setting
 Sociological Insights
 Policy Initiatives

BOXES

 TAKING SOCIOLOGY TO WORK*:
Amy Wang, Product Manager,
Norman International Company*
 ***SOCIOLOGY IN THE GLOBAL
COMMUNITY****: Charisma: The
Beatles and Maharishi Mahesh Yogi*

 RESEARCH TODAY*: Why Don't
More Young People Vote?*

 RESEARCH TODAY*: American
Indians: First Here, Among the Last
to Vote*

 RESEARCH TODAY*: Affirmative
Action*

KEY POINTS

The Political System: By **political system**, sociologists mean the social institution that is founded on a recognized set of procedures for implementing and achieving society's goals. Like religion and the family, the political system is a cultural universal: It is found in every society.

The Economic System: The term **economic system** refers to the social institution through which goods and services are produced, distributed, and consumed. As with social institutions such as the family, religion, and government, the economic system shapes other aspects of the social order and is in turn influenced by them.

Capitalism: **Capitalism** is an economic system in which the means of production are held largely in private hands, and the main incentive for economic activity is the accumulation of profit. In practice, capitalist systems vary in the degree to which the government regulates private ownership and economic activity. Contemporary capitalism features government regulation of economic relations and tolerance of monopolistic practices.

Socialism: Socialist theory was refined in the writings of Karl Marx and Friedrich Engels. Under **socialism**, the means of production and distribution in a society are collectively, rather than privately, owned. The basic objective of the economic system is to meet people's needs rather than to maximize profits. In theory, the wealth of the people as a collectivity is used to provide health care, housing, education, and other key services to each individual and family. Marx believed that each socialist state would eventually "wither away" and evolve into a communist state. As an ideal type, **communism** refers to an economic system under which all property is communally owned and no social distinctions are made based on people's ability to produce.

Capitalism in China: When the communists assumed leadership of China in 1949, they cast themselves as the champions of workers and peasants, and the enemies of those who exploited them—namely, landlords and capitalists. Profit making was outlawed, and by the 1960s, China was dominated by huge state-controlled enterprises. But the centralization of production did not work well economically. In the 1980s, the government eased restrictions against private enterprise somewhat, permitting the creation of small businesses. By the mid-1990s, party officials had begun to hand some ailing state-controlled businesses to over to private enterprises.

Power: Power lies at the heart of a political system. Max Weber defined **power** as the ability to exercise one's will over others. Power relations can involve large organizations, small groups, or even people in an intimate association. There are three basic sources of power within any political system: force, influence, and authority.

Types of Authority: Max Weber identified three ideal types of authority. In a political system based on **traditional authority**, legitimate power is conferred by custom and accepted practice. Authority does not rest in personal characteristics, technical competence, or even written law. Power made legitimate by law is known as **rational-legal authority**. Leaders derive their rational-legal authority from the written rules and regulations of political systems. The term **charismatic authority** refers to power made legitimate by a leader's exceptional personal or emotional appeal to his or her followers. Charisma lets a person lead or inspire without relying on set rules or traditions.

Types of Government: There are five basic types of government. A **monarchy** is a form of government headed by a single member of a royal family, usually a king, queen, or some other hereditary ruler. An **oligarchy** is a form of government in which a few individuals rule. A **dictatorship** is a government in which one person has nearly total power to make and enforce laws. Frequently, dictators develop such overwhelming control over people's lives that their governments are called **totalitarian**. **Democracy** means government by the people. The United States is commonly classified as a **representative democracy**, since the elected members of Congress and state legislators make our laws.

Elite and Pluralist Models of Power Relations: Who really holds power in the United States? Like others who hold an **elite model** of power relations, Karl Marx believed that society is ruled by a small group of individuals who share a common set of political and economic interests. Sociologist C. Wright Mills argued that power rested in the hands of a few, both inside and outside government—the **power elite**. Sociologist G. William Domhoff stresses the role played both by elites of the corporate community and by the leaders of policy-formation organizations, such as chambers of commerce and labor unions. Critics of the elite model of power relations insist that power is shared more widely than Marx, Mills, and Domhoff indicate. In their view, a **pluralist model** more accurately describes the nation's political system. In a pluralist model, many competing groups within the community have access to government so that no single group is dominant.

War, Peace, and Terrorism: Conflict is a central aspect of social relations. Too often it becomes ongoing and violent, engulfing innocent bystanders as well as intentional participants. **War** is defined as conflict between organizations that possess trained combat forces equipped with deadly weapons. Sociologists have considered **peace** both as the absence of war and as a proactive effort to develop cooperative relations among nations. Sociologists and other social scientists who draw on sociological theory and research have tried to identify conditions that deter war. **Terrorism** is the use or threat of violence against random or symbolic targets in pursuit of political aims.

The Changing Face of the Workforce: The number of Black, Latino, and Asian American workers continues to increase at a rate faster than the number of White workers. Increasingly, the workforce reflects the diversity of the population. This is due to ethnic minorities entering the labor force, and immigrants and their children moving from marginal jobs or employment in the informal economy to positions of greater visibility and responsibility. Interactionists note that people will find themselves supervising and being supervised by people very different from themselves.

Deindustrialization and Downsizing: The term **deindustrialization** refers to the systematic, widespread withdrawal of investment in basic aspects of productivity such as factories and plants. Some companies relocate from northeastern and midwestern states to southern states, while others relocate outside the United States to countries with lower rates of prevailing wages. The term **downsizing** was introduced in 1987 to refer to reductions taken in a company's workforce as part of deindustrialization. Viewed from a conflict perspective, the unprecedented attention given to downsizing in the mid-1990s reflected the continuing importance of social class in the United States. Conflict theorists note that job loss among workers has long been a feature of deindustrialization. But when large numbers of middle-class managers and other white-collar employees with substantial incomes began to be laid off, suddenly there was great concern in the media over downsizing.

Global Offshoring: U.S. firms have been outsourcing certain types of work for generations. The new trend toward offshoring carries this practice one step further, by transferring new types of work to foreign countries. Office and professional jobs are being exported, too, thanks to advanced telecommunications and the growth of skilled, English-speaking labor forces in developing nations with relatively low wage scales. Because offshoring, and outsourcing in general, tends to improve the efficiency of business operations, they can be viewed as functional to society. Conflict theorists question whether this aspect of globalization furthers social inequality.

KEY TERMS

Briefly define or identify the following terms in the spaces provided below. The definitions of these terms can be found later in this chapter of the study guide.

Political system	Capitalism
Economic system	Laissez-faire
Industrial society	Monopoly

Socialism	Oligarchy
Communism	Dictatorship
Informal economy	Totalitarianism
Politics	Democracy
Power	Representative democracy
Force	Elite model
Influence	Power elite
Authority	Pluralist model
Traditional authority	War
Rational-legal authority	Peace
Charismatic authority	Terrorism
Monarchy	Deindustrialization

Affirmative action	Offshoring
Downsizing	

SELF-TEST

MODIFIED TRUE/FALSE QUESTIONS: If the statement below is true, write "true" in the space provided. If the statement is false, briefly correct the error.

1. In reality, the economy of every industrial society includes elements of both capitalism and socialism.

2. In the informal economy, transfers of money, goods, and services are reported to the government, but in approximate numbers and without receipts.

3. Following several decades of socialism, the Chinese government began to allow private businesses to emerge in the 1980s.

4. The shift to a market economy in China has resulted in great advances in economic status for women.

5. Max Weber developed a classification system regarding authority in which he distinguished among rational, traditional-legal, and charismatic types of authority.

6.   In societies based on rational-legal authority, legitimate power is conferred by custom and accepted practice.

7.   In the United States, voter turnout has been particularly high among younger adults.

8.   Karl Marx believed that society is ruled by a small group of individuals who share a common set of political and economic interests.

9.   In many respects, the power elite model developed by C. Wright Mills is similar to the work of Max Weber.

10.   Robert Dahl's study of decision making in New Haven, Connecticut, lends support to the power elite model of social power.

11.   One critique of the pluralist model focuses on the possible power of elites to keep certain matters out of the realm of government debate.

12.   While terrorists may wish to keep secret their individual identities, they want their political messages and goals to receive as much publicity as possible.

13.   Although there are significant racial and ethnic differences in people's views on affirmative action, gender differences are largely absent.

14.   Viewed from a functionalist perspective, the unprecedented attention given to downsizing in the mid-1990s reflected the continuing importance of social class in the United States.

15.   Outsourcing is a relatively new practice among U.S. firms.

MULTIPLE-CHOICE QUESTIONS: Read each question carefully and then select the best answer.

1.   Which of the following is a cultural universal?
   a. religion
   b. the political system
   c. the family
   d. all of the above

2.   Which two basic types of economic system distinguish contemporary industrial societies?
   a. capitalism and communism
   b. capitalism and socialism
   c. socialism and communism
   d. capitalism and dictatorships

3.   Which of the following is an economic system that is typically found in contemporary societies?
   a. socialism
   b. feudalism
   c. slavery
   d. all of the above

4.   The principle of laissez-faire was expounded and endorsed by the British economist

    a. John Maynard Keynes.

    b. Adam Smith.

    c. Paul Samuelson.

    d. Arthur Scargill.

5.   Which sociological perspective points out that while pure monopolies are not a basic element of the economy of the United States, competition is much more restricted than one might expect in what is called a free enterprise system?

    a. the functionalist perspective

    b. the conflict perspective

    c. the interactionist perspective

    d. labeling theory

6.   Socialist theory was refined in the writings of Karl Marx and

    a. Émile Durkheim.

    b. Adam Smith.

    c. Friedrich Engels.

    d. the Marx Brothers.

7.   Which of the following is NOT an example of the informal economy?

    a. trading a haircut for a computer lesson

    b. selling illegal drugs

    c. working for a major corporation as a computer programmer

    d. offering child care out of a private home without reporting the income to the IRS

8.   Political scientist Harold Lasswell defined *politics* as:

    a. the struggle for power and authority.

    b. the allocation of valued resources.

    c. who gets what, when, and how.

    d. a cultural universal.

9.   What are the three basic sources of power within any political system?

a. force, influence, and authority

b. force, influence, and democracy

c. force, legitimacy, and charisma

d. influence, charisma, and bureaucracy

10. Which of the following is NOT part of the classification system of authority that was developed by Max Weber?

a. traditional authority

b. pluralist authority

c. rational-legal authority

d. charismatic authority

11. A king or queen is accepted as ruler of a nation simply by virtue of having inherited the crown. This is an example of

a. totalitarianism.

b. charismatic authority.

c. traditional authority.

d. rational-legal authority.

12. The authority of Congress and the authority of the president of the United States are legitimized by the Constitution. This is an example of

a. political efficacy.

b. charismatic authority.

c. traditional authority.

d. rational-legal authority.

13. Which of the following can be classified as a charismatic leader?

a. Joan of Arc

b. Malcolm X

c. Adolf Hitler

d. all of the above

14. Totalitarian states typically control which of the following institutions?

a. the family

b. the economy

c. politics

d. all of the above

15.   The U.S. government can best be described as a(n):
  a. oligarchy.
  b. dictatorship.
  c. democracy.
  d. representative democracy.

16.   Almost _____ percent of eligible voters in the United States went to the polls in the presidential election of 1896 as compared to less than _____ percent in the 2000 election.
  a. 75; 25
  b. 80; 47
  c. 15; 10
  d. 73; 70

17.   The popular explanation for voter apathy among the young is that:
  a. they must first register to vote.
  b. young people are alienated from the political system.
  c. young people feel unmoved by local issues.
  d. potential voters are no longer greeted by the political party faithful.

18.   In C. Wright Mills's power elite model, which of the following is NOT at the top of the power structure in the United States?
  a. the corporate rich
  b. the leaders of the executive branch of government
  c. the heads of the military
  d. the members of the Supreme Court and legislative leaders

19.   Which of the following social scientists is associated with the pluralist model of power relations?
  a. Robert Dahl
  b. C. Wright Mills
  c. G. William Domhoff
  d. Max Weber

20.   Which of the following is NOT one of the approaches that sociologists take in the study of war?
  a. a global view
  b. a nation-state view
  c. a polarized view
  d. a micro view

21. Which of the following are conditions that sociologists have identified as helping to deter war?
    a. international trade
    b. immigration and foreign-exchange programs
    c. activities of international charities and NGOs
    d. all of the above

22   Sociologists and labor specialists foresee a workforce increasingly composed of
    a. women.
    b. racial minorities.
    c. ethnic minorities.
    d. all of the above

23. The systematic, widespread withdrawal of investment in basic aspects of productivity such as factories and plants is called
    a. deindustrialization.
    b. downsizing.
    c. postindustrialization.
    d. deconstruction.

24. In which of these states have residents voted for measures aimed at abolishing affirmative action?
    a. Washington
    b. California
    c. Iowa
    d. both a and b

25. The most recent trend in offshoring is that _____ jobs are being transferred to foreign contractors.
    a. manufacturing
    b. office and professional
    c. post-modern
    d. agricultural

FILL-IN QUESTIONS: Fill in the blank spaces in the sentences below with the correct words. Where two or more words are required, there will be a corresponding number of blank spaces.

1.   A(n) _____ society depends on mechanization to produce its goods and services.

2.   Under _____ as an ideal type, government rarely takes over ownership of an entire industry.

3.   _____ is an economic system under which all property is communally owned and no social distinctions are made based on people's ability to produce.

4.   Capitalism and socialism serve as _____ _____ of economic systems; the economy of each industrial society includes certain elements of both these types of economic systems.

5.   _____ is the actual or threatened use of coercion to impose one's will on others.

6.   Joan of Arc, Mahatma Gandhi, Malcolm X, and Martin Luther King, Jr., are all examples of _____ leaders.

7.   In most of today's _____, kings and queens have little practical power.

8.   Studies reveal that only _____ percent of the people in the United States belong to a political club or organization.

9.   G. William Domhoff noted that in the electoral arena, two different coalitions have exercised influence. One of these coalitions, the _____-_____ coalition, is based in unions, local environmental organizations, some minority-group communities, liberal churches, and the university and arts communities.

10.   Robert Dahl argued for the _____ model of power.

11.   Advocates of the _____ model suggest that conflicting groups within the community have access to government so that no single group is dominant.

12.   _____ is the use or threat of violence against random or symbolic targets in pursuit of political aims.

13.   While _____ often involves relocation, in some instances it takes the form of corporate restructuring, as companies seek to reduce costs in the face of growing worldwide competition.

14.   The term _____ was introduced in 1987 and refers to reductions taken in a company's workforce as part of deindustrialization.

15.   The annual turnover rate in offshored, high-tech jobs in India is more than _____ percent.

UNDERSTANDING SOCIAL POLICY: Each of the following questions is based on material that appears in the social policy section on "Global Offshoring." Write a brief answer to each question in the space provided below.

1.   What is the distinction between outsourcing and offshoring?

2.   How extensive is the practice of offshoring?

3.   How do functionalists and conflict theorists view global offshoring?

DEFINITIONS OF KEY TERMS

Political system: The social institution that is founded on a recognized set of procedures for implementing and achieving society's goals.

Economic system: The social institution through which goods and services are produced, distributed, and consumed.

Industrial society: A society that depends on mechanization to produce its goods and services.

Capitalism: An economic system in which the means of production are held largely in private hands and the main incentive for economic activity is the accumulation of profits.

Laissez-faire: A form of capitalism under which people compete freely, with minimal government intervention in the economy.

Monopoly: Control of a market by a single business firm.

Socialism: An economic system under which the means of production and distribution are collectively owned.

Communism: As an ideal type, an economic system under which all property is communally owned and no social distinctions are made on the basis of people's ability to produce.

Informal economy: Transfers of money, goods, or services that are not reported to the government.

Politics: In Harold Lasswell's words, "who gets what, when, and how."

Power: The ability to exercise one's will over others.

Force: The actual or threatened use of coercion to impose one's will on others.

Influence: The exercise of power through a process of persuasion.

Authority: Institutionalized power that is recognized by the people over whom it is exercised.

Traditional authority: Legitimate power conferred by custom and accepted practice.

Rational-legal authority: Power made legitimate by law.

Charismatic authority: Power made legitimate by a leader's exceptional personal or emotional appeal to his or her followers.

Monarchy: A form of government headed by a single member of a royal family, usually a king, queen, or some other hereditary ruler.

Oligarchy: A form of government in which a few individuals rule.

Dictatorship: A government in which one person has nearly total power to make and enforce laws.

Totalitarianism: Virtually complete government control and surveillance over all aspects of a society's social and political life.

Democracy: In a literal sense, government by the people.

Representative democracy: A form of government in which certain individuals are selected to speak for the people.

Elite model: A view of society as being ruled by a small group of individuals who share a common set of political and economic interests.

Power elite: A small group of military, industrial, and government leaders who control the fate of the United States.

Pluralist model: A view of society in which many competing groups within the community have access to government, so that no single group is dominant.

War: Conflict between organizations that possess trained combat forces equipped with deadly weapons.

Peace: The absence of war, or more broadly, a proactive effort to develop cooperative relations among nations.

Terrorism: The use or threat of violence against random or symbolic targets in pursuit of political aims.

Deindustrialization: The systematic, widespread withdrawal of investment in basic aspects of productivity such as factories and plants.

Downsizing: Reductions taken in a company's workforce as part of deindustrialization.

Off-shoring The transfer of work to foreign contractors.

ANSWERS TO SELF-TEST

Modified True/False Questions

1. True

2. The informal economy consists of transfers of money, goods, and services that are not reported to the government.

3. True

4. Scholars are still waiting to see whether Chinese women will maintain the progress they began under Communism.

5. Max Weber developed a classification system regarding authority in which he distinguished among traditional, rational-legal, and charismatic types of authority.

6. In societies based on traditional authority, legitimate power is conferred by custom and accepted practice.

7. In the United States, voter turnout has been particularly low among younger adults.

8. True

9. The power elite model developed by C. Wright Mills is, in many respects, similar to the work of Karl Marx.

10. Robert Dahl's study lends support to the pluralist model of social power.

11. True

12. True

13. While 60 percent of White women in a 2004 survey approved of affirmative action in college admissions, the approval rate for White men was only 49 percent.

14. Viewed from a conflict perspective, the unprecedented attention given to downsizing in the mid-1990s reflected the continuing importance of social class in the United States.

15. U.S. firms have been outsourcing certain types of work for generations.

Multiple-Choice Questions

1. d	10. b	19. a
2. b	11. c	20. c
3. a	12. d	21. d
4. b	13. d	22. d
5. b	14. d	23. a
6. c	15. d	24. d
7. c	16. b	25. b
8. c	17. b	
9. a	18. d	

Fill-In Questions

1. industrial	9. liberal-labor
2. capitalism	10. pluralist
3. Communism	11. pluralist
4. ideal types	12. Terrorism
5. Force	13. deindustrialization
6. charismatic	14. downsizing
7. monarchies	15. 50
8. 8	

Understanding Social Policy: Global Offshoring

1. U.S. firms have been outsourcing certain types of work for generations. The new trend toward offshoring carries this practice one step further, by transferring other

types of work to foreign contractors. Office and professional jobs are now being transferred as well.

2. Today, when you call a toll-free number to reach a customer-service representative, chances are that the person who answers the phone will not be speaking from the United States. Estimates are that by the year 2008, 4.1 million service jobs will be performed in lower-wage countries for customers in higher-wage economies.

3. Because offshoring (and outsourcing in general) tends to improve the efficiency of business operations, it can be viewed as functional to society. But conflict theorists question whether this aspect of globalization furthers global inequality.

15 HEALTH, MEDICINE, AND THE ENVIRONMENT

Culture and Health

Sociological Perspectives on Health and Illness
    Functionalist Approach
    Conflict Approach
    Interactionist Approach
    Labeling Approach

Social Epidemiology and Health
    Social Class
    Race and Ethnicity
    Gender
    Age

Health Care in the United States
    A Historical View
    Physicians, Nurses, and Patients
    Alternatives to Traditional Health Care
    The Role of the Government

Sociological Perspectives on the Environment
    Human Ecology
    Conflict View of the Environment
    Environmental Justice

Environmental Problems
    Air Pollution
    Water Pollution
    Global Warming
    The Impact of Globalization

Social Policy and Health: The AIDS Crisis
    The Issue
    The Setting
    Sociological Insights
    Policy Initiatives

BOXES
    PHOTO ESSAY: *What is Medical Care?*
    RESEARCH TODAY: *To Inform or Not to Inform? How Race and Ethnicity Affect Views of Patient Autonomy*
    RESEARCH TODAY: *Medical Apartheid*
    TAKING SOCIOLOGY TO WORK: *Lola Adedokun, Independent Consultant, Health Care Research*
    SOCIOLOGY IN THE GLOBAL COMMUNITY: *The Mysterious Fall of the Nacirema*

KEY POINTS

Functionalist Approach to Health and Illness: The **sick role** refers to societal expectations about the attitudes and behavior of a person viewed as being ill. Sociologist Talcott Parsons, well-known for his contributions to functionalist theory, outlined the behavior required of people considered "sick." According to Parsons, physicians function as "gatekeepers" for the sick role, either verifying a patient's condition as "illness" or designating the patient as "recovered."

Conflict Approach to Health and Illness: Conflict theorists use the term medicalization of society to refer to the growing role of medicine as a major institution of social control. Medicine serves as an agent of social control by retaining absolute jurisdiction over many health care procedures. Viewed from a conflict perspective, there are glaring inequities in health care delivery in the United States. For example, poor areas tend to be underserved because medical services concentrate where people are wealthy. Similarly, from a global perspective, there are obvious inequities in health care delivery.

Interactionist Approach to Health and Illness: In examining health, illness, and medicine as a social institution, interactionists generally focus on micro-level study of the roles played by health care professionals and patients. They emphasize that the patient should not always be viewed as passive. Sometimes patients play an active role in health care by *failing* to follow a physician's advice.

Labeling Approach to Health and Illness: Labeling theorists suggest that the designation "healthy" or "ill" generally involves social definition by others. Just as police officers, judges, and other regulators of social control have the power to define certain people as criminals, health care professionals (especially physicians) have the power to define certain people as "sick." Moreover, like labels that suggest nonconformity or criminality, labels that are associated with illness commonly reshape how others treat us and how we see ourselves. Our society attaches serious consequences to labels that suggest less than perfect physical or mental health.

Social Epidemiology and Health: **Social epidemiology** is the study of the distribution of disease, impairment, and general health status across a population. Studies in the United States and other countries have consistently shown that people in the lower classes have higher rates of mortality and disability. The poor economic and environmental conditions of groups such as African Americans, Hispanics, and Native Americans are manifested in high morbidity and mortality rates for these groups. A large body of research indicates that in comparison with men, women experience a higher prevalence of many illnesses, though they tend to live longer.

Health Care in the United States: Historically, health care in the U.S. was characterized by self-help, prevention, a variety of approaches to practice and types of practitioners. With the growth of the American Medical Association, the medical model became standard by the 1920s. Critics of the medical model assert that medical school emphasizes technical and clinical skill, dehumanizing doctor- patient relationships. Nurses are expected to remain subordinate. Gender appears to contribute to lower status of female physicians. **Holistic medicine**, in which the practitioner considers the physical, mental, emotional, and spiritual characteristics of the patient, is an increasing challenge to the medical establishment. Approximately one-third of U.S. adults use some type of alternative therapy. However, most alternative therapies are not covered by health insurance. Government funding, especially via Medicare and Medicaid payments, has had a significant effect on the health care system.

Human Ecology: Human ecology is concerned with the interrelationships between people and their environment. Emphasis is placed on three relationships: a) the environment provides people the resources necessary for life, b) the environment serves as a waste repository, c) the environment "houses" our species.

Conflict View of Environmental Issues: World systems analysis shows how a growing share of the human and natural resources of the developing countries is being redistributed to the core industrialized nations. This process only intensifies the destruction of natural resources in poorer regions of the world. From a conflict perspective, less affluent nations are being forced to exploit their mineral deposits, forests, and fisheries in order to meet their debt obligations.

Environmental Justice: is a legal strategy based on claims that racial minorities are subjected disproportionately to environmental hazards, and that the poor and oppressed continue to bear the brunt of environmental pollution.

Environmental Problems: World population growth and increasing use of technological innovations are significant causes of environmental problems. More than 1 billion people on the planet are exposed to potentially health-damaging levels of air pollution. Throughout the United States, streams, rivers, and lakes have been polluted by the dumping of waste materials by both industries and local governments. Global warming refers to the significant rise of the earth's temperature caused by the release of industrial gases like carbon dioxide. World systems analysis suggests that the challenge of global warming is tied to global inequality.

The AIDS Crisis: AIDS caught major social institutions—particularly the government, the health care system, and the economy—by surprise when it was noticed initially by medical practitioners in the 1970s. As functionalists would predict, new social networks have emerged for dealing with the AIDS crisis. Self-help groups, especially in the gay communities of major cities, have been established to care for the sick, educate the healthy, and lobby for more responsive public policies. The label of "person with AIDS" or "HIV positive" often functions as a master status that stigmatizes those so labeled.

KEY TERMS

Briefly define or identify the following terms in the spaces provided below. The definitions of these terms can be found later in this chapter of the study guide.

Culture-bound syndrome	Morbidity rate
Health	Mortality rate
Sick role	Prevalence
Brain drain	*Curanderismo*
Infant mortality rate	Holistic medicine
Social epidemiology	Human ecology
Incidence	Environmental justice

SELF-TEST

MODIFIED TRUE/FALSE QUESTIONS: If the statement below is true, write "true" in the space provided. If the statement is false, briefly correct the error.

1. In the United States, anorexia nervosa is an example of a culture-bound syndrome that is receiving increasing attention.

2.   Health is defined as the absence of illness or disease.

3.   According to functionalists, the doctor-nurse game refers to the role people plays
        in order to fulfill their obligation to get well.

4.   Conflict theorists use the term *medicalization of society* to refer to the growing
        role of medicine as a major institution of social control.

5.   The infant mortality rate of the United States is lower than that of any other
        nation.

6.   Labeling theorists argue that labels associated with illness commonly reshape how
        others treat us and how we see ourselves.

7.   Prevalence refers to the total number of cases of a specific disorder that exist at a
        given time.

8.   Lack of health insurance causes less access to good care, but in the final analysis,
        lack of insurance is not life-threatening.

9.   Medical apartheid refers to the South African practice of providing inferior health
        care to racial minorities.

10.   Compared to other groups, the elderly are more likely to suffer from chronic illnesses.

11.   Acupuncture, herbal remedies, massage, nutrition, exercise, and visualization are all examples of alternatives to traditional health care in the U.S.

12.   According to the conflict perspective, less affluent countries are forced to exploit their natural resources to the point of environmental destruction.

13.   NIMBY protests are typical of how lower-status Americans historically prevented being subjected to disproportionate exposure to environmental hazards.

14.   In 2008, only forty-nine percent of adults said that protection of the environment should be given priority by the government.

15.   Most Americans do not believe in global warming.

MULTIPLE-CHOICE QUESTIONS: Read each question carefully and then select the best answer.

1.   Being healthy is
        a. not having a diagnosed disease.

    b. relative, depending on a variety of criteria.

    c. absolute – either you have a diagnosis or you don't.

    d. means the same thing in all cultures.

2.   In 1974, members of the American Psychiatric Association voted to drop
_____ from the standard manual of mental disorders.

    a. premenstrual syndrome

    b. homosexuality

    c. schizophrenia

    d. hyperactivity

3.   According to conflict theory,

    a. medicine is primarily a healing profession.

    b. medicine is an agent of social control.

    c. medicine safeguards its monopoly on the provision of health care by defining other models and therapists and being outside of acceptable care.

    d. b and c.

4.   Which of the following is a criticism of the sick role?

    a. Patients' judgments regarding their own state of health may be related to their gender, age, social class, and ethnic group.

    b. The sick role may be more applicable to people experiencing short-term illnesses than to those with recurring long-term illnesses.

    c. Even simple factors, such as whether a person is employed or not, seem to affect willingness to assume the sick role.

    d. all of the above

5.   Which sociological perspective emphasizes that a patient should not always be viewed as passive, but instead as someone who often plays an active role in his or her health care?

    a. the functionalist perspective

    b. the conflict perspective

    c. the interactionist perspective

    d. labeling theory

6.   In examining health, illness, and medicine as a social institution, which sociological perspective generally focuses on micro-level study of the roles played by health care professionals and patients?

    a. the functionalist perspective

    b. the conflict perspective

    c. the interactionist perspective

    d. labeling theory

7.   According to (the) _____, we can view a variety of life experiences as illnesses or not.

    a. functionalist perspective

    b. conflict perspective

    c. interactionist perspective

    d. labeling theory

8.   _____ theory emphasizes that inequities in health care result in serious consequences such as higher infant mortality rates among underserved populations.

    a. Functionalist

    b. Conflict

    c. Interactionist

    d. Labeling

9.   When a diagnosis-related label such as "person with AIDS" overshadows all other aspects of a person's life, the label functions as a/an _____.

    a. master status.

    b. incidence.

    c. congenital disease.

    d. prejudice.

10.   While mortality rate refers to the incidence of death in a particular population, morbidity refers to

    a. the incidence of mental illness such as depression in a given population.

    b. the incidence of deaths in hospitals.

    c. the incidence of people who are overweight in a particular population.

    d. the incidence of disease in a given population.

11.   Compared with Whites, Blacks have higher death rates from

    a. heart disease.

    b. diabetes.

    c. cancer.

    d. all of the above

12. Crowded housing, stress, poor nutrition, lack of information, financial strain, poor healthcare in childhood are all causes of health problems among
    a. members of racial minority groups.
    b. members of ethnic minority groups.
    c. women.
    d. low-income people in the United States.

13. A study of male and female residents suggests that the increasing number of female physicians may alter the traditional doctor-patient relationship because
    a. female residents are more interested in technical competence than male residents.
    b. female residents spend more time with patients than male residents.
    c. female residents are more likely to be motivated by the intellectual challenges than male residents.
    d. female residents demand fewer hours of on-call duty in order to meet their family responsibilities.

14. Today, patients are getting information on health care issues from
    _____ .
    a. the Internet.
    b. pharmaceutical companies' TV advertisements.
    c. pharmaceutical firm's magazine advertisements.
    d. all of the above.

15. Geographic disparities in health care resources in evidenced in the disproportionately favorable availability of physicians to residents of the
    a. northwestern United States.
    b. northeastern United States.
    c. southwestern United States.
    d. southeastern United States.

16. Between 1980 and 1997, health care costs in the United States
    a. quadrupled.
    b. tripled.
    c. doubled.

d. remained about the same.

17. Which of the following is least likely to be funded by a grant from the NIH Office of Alternative Medicine?
    a. IV pharmaceutics for cancer patients
    b. the use of visualization to fight cancer
    c. the use of massage and nutrition to help patients cope with the stress of other cancer therapies
    d. herbal remedies

18. _____ theorists point out that blaming "food hungry" nations for environmental problems amounts to ethnocentrism on the part of "energy hungry" nations.
    a. Functionalist
    b. Conflict
    c. Interactionist
    d. Labeling

19. According to Allan Schnaiberg, environmental troubles are caused by increasing demand for profits by affluent customers, supporting a
    a. vicious cycle of health problems.
    b. treadmill of production.
    c. dysfunctional adaptation to the environment.
    d. none of the above

20. The human ecology approach to the environment considers all of the following relationships except.
    a. the environment is appropriately seen as having humans at the top of the web of life.
    b. the environment "houses" our species.
    c. the environment provides the resources necessary for life.
    d. the environment serves as a waste repository.

21. The World Health Organization estimates that up to 700,000 deaths per year could be eliminated by reducing
    a. water pollution.
    b. environmental degradation.
    c. traffic.

d. smog.

22.   Worldwide, over _____ people lack a safe and adequate water supply.
   a. 50 million
   b. 500 million
   c. over one billion
   d. over two billion

23.   In 2006, the United States was the largest emitter of carbon dioxide from fossil fuels. Recent research shows that _____ has now taken the lead.
   a. India
   b. China
   c. Mexico
   d. Australia

24.   According to _____ theory, AIDS could lead to a more conservative sexual climate as people become more cautious about becoming involved with new partners and more concerned with 'safe sex' when they do.
   a. functionalist
   b. conflict
   c. interactionist
   d. labeling

25.   AIDS is most prevalent in the areas of the world that are least equipped to deal with such a disease, namely
   a. India
   b. Southeast Asia
   c. Mexico
   d. Sub-Saharan Africa

FILL-IN QUESTIONS: Fill in the blank spaces in the sentences below with the correct words. Where two or more words are required, there will be a corresponding number of blank spaces.

1. Japanese society frowns on organ donations, therefore people in Japan are less likely to receive transplant surgery. This is an example of how _____ affects health.

2. From a(n) _____ perspective, "being sick" must be controlled so as to ensure that not too many people are released from their societal responsibilities at any one time.

3. According to Talcott Parsons, physicians function as "_____" for the sick role, either verifying a patient's condition as "illness" or designating the patient as "recovered."

4. According to the _____ approach, patients are not just passive recipients of health care, but rather play an active role in seeking, accepting, or rejecting medical care.

5. _____ theorists suggest that the designation of a person as "healthy" or "ill" generally involves social definition by others.

6. Women are far more likely than men to develop breast cancer; in other words, they have a higher _____ _____ for breast cancer than men do.

7. Low income leads to poor health, which then hinders upward mobility in a _____ _____.

8. As more women feel pressured to use medical treatments in the pursuit of a more beautiful appearance, conflict theorists suggest that these women are falling victim to the _____ _____ _____.

9. People who are 75 and older are _____ times more likely to use health services and be hospitalized than younger people.

10. _____ _____ refers practice that considers the mental, emotional, and spiritual well-being of the patient as well as the physical.

11. The immigration to the United States and other industrialized nations of skilled workers, professionals, and technicians who are desperately needed by their home countries is known as the _____ _____.

12.   Regarding environmental problems, three broad areas of concern stand out: _____ pollution, _____ pollution, and the impact of _____.

13.   According to the _____ _____ approach, the environment provides the resources needed to sustain life while housing our species and being a repository for wastes.

14.   The Warren County struggle for environmental clean-up is and example of the _____ _____ strategy.

15.   Given increasing population and increasing pollution, competition for clean _____ is intense.

UNDERSTANDING SOCIAL POLICY: Each of the following questions is based on material that appears in the social policy section on "The AIDS Crisis." Write a brief answer to each question in the space provided below.

1.   Why is there such a strong stigma attached to infection with the HIV virus and to AIDS?

2.   What observations have been made from the conflict perspective regarding the response by policy makers to the AIDS crisis?

3.   Regarding the micro level of social interaction, what did sociologists predict about the AIDS crisis?

DEFINITIONS OF KEY TERMS

Culture-bound syndrome: A disease or illness that cannot be understood apart from its specific social context.

Health: As defined by the World Health Organization, a state of complete physical, mental, and social well-being, and not merely the absence of disease and infirmity.

Sick role: Societal expectations about the attitudes and behavior of a person viewed as being ill.

Brain drain: The immigration to the United States and other industrialized nations of skilled workers, professionals, and technicians who are desperately needed in their home countries.

Infant mortality rate: The number of deaths of infants under one year old per 1,000 live births in a given year.

Social epidemiology: The study of the distribution of disease, impairment, and general health status across a population.

Incidence: The number of new cases of a specific disorder that occur within a given population during a stated period.

Morbidity rate: The incidence of disease in a given population.

Mortality rate: The incidence of death in a given population.

Prevalence: The total number of cases of a specific disorder that exist at a given time.

Curanderismo: Latino folk medicine, a form of holistic health care and healing.

Holistic medicine: Therapies in which the health care practitioner considers the person's physical, mental, emotional and spiritual characteristics.

Human ecology: An area of study that is concerned with the interrelationships between people and their environment.

Environmental Justice: A legal strategy based on claims that racial minorities are subjected disproportionately to environmental hazards.

ANSWERS TO SELF-TEST

Modified True/False Questions

1. True
2. Health is defined as a state of complete physical, mental, and social well-being, and not merely the absence of disease and infirmity.
3. According to functionalists, the sick role refers to the role people play in order to fulfill their obligation to get well.
4. True

5. Forty-two nations have lower infant mortality rates than that of the United States.
6. True
7. True
8. Lack of health insurance causes less access to good care, and accounted for 22,000 deaths in 2006.
9. Medical apartheid refers to the practice of providing inferior health care to African Americans.
10. True
11. True
12. True
13. The environmental justice movement is a relatively recent legal strategy used by minority group members to prevent disproportionate exposure to environmental hazards.
14. True
15. Sixty-three percent of Americans believe that the effects of global warming are already manifest, or that they will occur within 5 years.

Multiple-Choice Questions

1. d	10. c	19. b
2. d	11. a	20. d
3. d	12. d	21. c
4. a	13. c	22. c
5. a	14. b	23. d
6. d	15. a	24. b
7. a	16. b	25. d
8. c	17. b	
9. c	18. d	

Fill-In Questions

1. culture	9. five
2. Functionalist	10. holistic
3. gatekeepers	11. brain drain
4. interactionist	12. air, water, global warming
5. Labeling	13. human ecology
6. morbidity rate	14. environmental justice
7. vicious cycle	15. water
8. medicalization of society	

Understanding Social Policy: The AIDS Crisis

1. People who have AIDS or who are infected with the HIV virus actually face a powerful dual stigma. Not only are they associated with a lethal and contagious disease, but they also have a disease that disproportionately afflicts already stigmatized groups, such as gay males and drug users.

2. Viewed from a conflict perspective, policymakers were slow to respond to the AIDS crisis because those in high-risk groups—gay men and IV drug users—were comparatively powerless. This linkage with stigmatized groups delayed recognition of the severity of the AIDS epidemic; the media took little interest in the disease until it seemed to be spreading beyond the gay community.

3. On the micro level of social interaction, observers widely forecast that AIDS would lead to a more conservative sexual climate—among both homosexuals and heterosexuals—in which people would be much more cautious about becoming involved with new sexual partners.

Social Movements
  Relative Deprivation Approach
  Resource Mobilization Approach
  Gender and Social Movements

Communications and the Globalization of Social Movements
  New Social Movements

Theories of Social Change
  Evolutionary Theory
  Functionalist Theory
  Conflict Theory

Resistance to Social Change
  Economic and Cultural Factors
  Resistance to Technology

Global Social Change

Technology and the Future
  Computer Technology
  Privacy and Censorship in a Global Village
  Biotechnology and the Gene Pool

Social Policy and Globalization: Transnationals
  The Issue
  The Setting
  Sociological Insights
  Policy Initiatives

BOXES
  RESEARCH TODAY: *Organizing for Controversy on the Web*
  RESEARCH TODAY: *The Internet's Global Profile*
  SOCIOLOGY IN THE GLOBAL COMMUNITY: *One Laptop per Child*

KEY POINTS

Social Movements: Sociologists use the term **social movement** to refer to organized collective activities to bring about or resist fundamental change in an existing group or society. Social movements imply the existence of conflict, but we can also analyze their activities from a functionalist perspective, which views social movements as training grounds for leaders of the political establishment.

Relative Deprivation: The term **relative deprivation** is defined as the conscious feeling of a negative discrepancy between legitimate expectations and present actualities. It may be characterized by scarcity rather than a complete lack of necessities. A relatively deprived person is dissatisfied because he or she feels downtrodden relative to some appropriate reference group. A group will not mobilize into a social movement unless there is a shared perception that members can end their relative deprivation only through collective action.

Resource Mobilization: The term **resource mobilization** is used to refer to the ways in which a social movement utilizes such resources as money, political influence, access to the media, and personnel. Leadership is a central factor in the mobilization of the discontented into social movements. Karl Marx recognized the importance of recruitment when he called on workers to become aware of their oppressed status and to develop a class consciousness.

Communication and Globalization: Global text messaging and the Internet enable social activists to reach a global audience almost instantaneously and at very low cost. Organizers of social movements can recruit people without any direct interaction.

New Social Movements: The term **new social movements** refers to organized collective activities that address values and social identities as well as improvements in the quality of life. Educated, middle-class people are significantly represented in some of these new social movements, such as the women's movement and the movement for lesbian and gay rights.

Evolutionary Theory: **Evolutionary theory** views society as moving in a definite direction. Early evolutionary theorists generally agreed that society was inevitably progressing to a higher state. August Comte saw human societies as moving forward in their thinking from mythology to the scientific method. Émile Durkheim maintained that society progressed from simple to more complex forms of social organization.

The Functionalist View of Change: Talcott Parsons, a leading proponent of functionalist theory, viewed society as being in a natural state of equilibrium. According to his equilibrium model, as changes occur in one part of society, adjustments must be made in other parts. Though Parsons's approach explicitly incorporates the evolutionary notion of continuing progress, the dominant theme in this model is balance and stability.

The Conflict View of Change: Conflict theorists contend that social institutions and practices persist because powerful groups have the ability to maintain the status quo. Change has crucial significance, since it is needed to correct social injustices and inequalities. In contrast to functionalists' emphasis on stability, Karl Marx argued that conflict is a normal and desirable aspect of social change. In fact, change must be encouraged as a means of eliminating social inequality.

Resistance to Social Change: Efforts to promote social change are likely to meet with resistance. Social economist Thorstein Veblen coined the term **vested interests** to refer to those people or groups who will suffer in the event of social change. In general, those with a disproportionate share of society's wealth, status, and power have a vested interest in preserving the status quo.

Global Social Change: In this era of massive social, political, and economic change on a global scale, is it possible to predict change? In her presidential address to the American Sociological Association, Maureen Hallinan cautioned that we need to move beyond the restrictive models of social change—the linear view of evolutionary theory and the assumptions about equilibrium in functionalist theory.

Computer Technology: We are living in an era of explosive growth and change in computer technology. However, the benefits of advancing technology are not equally distributed in the US or worldwide. There is a global problem of unequal distribution of access to technology and the information, education, commerce tied to it.

Privacy and Censorship in a Global Village: The complex issue of privacy and censorship in this technological age can be considered an illustration of culture lag, in which the material culture (the technology) is changing faster than the nonmaterial culture (norms controlling the technology). Functionalists point to the manifest function of the Internet in its ability to facilitate communications. They also identify the latent function of providing a forum for groups with few resources to communicate with the masses. Conflict theorists note that there is ever-present danger that a society's most powerful groups will use technological advances to invade the privacy of the less powerful.

Biotechnology and the Gene Pool: George Ritzer's concept of McDonaldization applies to the entire area of biotechnology. Just as the fast-food concept has permeated society, no phase of life now seems exempt from therapeutic or medical intervention. Today's biotechnology holds itself out as totally beneficial to human beings, but it is in constant need of monitoring,

Transnationals: The labor market has become an increasingly global one. Sociologists are finding that new technologies that facilitate international travel and communication are accelerating the transnational movement of workers. Functionalists see the free flow of immigrants as one way for economies to maximize their use of human labor. Conflict theorists charge that globalization and international migration have increased the economic gulf between developed and developing nations.

KEY TERMS

Briefly define or identify the following terms in the spaces provided below. The definitions of these terms can be found later in this chapter of the study guide.

Social change	Evolutionary theory
Social movement	Equilibrium model
Relative deprivation	Vested interests
Resource mobilization	Culture lag
False consciousness	Luddites
New social movement	Environmental justice
Transnational	

SELF-TEST

MODIFIED TRUE/FALSE QUESTIONS: If the statement below is true, write "true" in the space provided. If the statement is false, briefly correct the error.

1.   Poland's Lech Walesa, Russia's Boris Yeltsin, and the Czech Republic's Vaclav Havel led protest movements against Communist rule, and subsequently became leaders of their countries' governments.

2.   A disadvantaged group will not mobilize into a social movement unless there is a shared perception that its relative deprivation can be ended only through collective action.

3.   Since social movements tend to be progressive, women are often able to assume leadership positions in social movement organizations.

4.   Whereas traditional views of social movements tended to emphasize resource mobilization on a broad, global level, new social movements theory offers a local perspective on social and political activism.

5.   India's SSKKMS social movement had a fairly typical leadership core comprised of middle-class men.

6.   Early evolutionary theorists generally agreed that society was inevitably progressing to a higher state.

7. Talcott Parsons' approach to social change explicitly rejects the evolutionary notion of continuing progress.

8. As noted by critics, the functionalist approach places substantial emphasis on the use of coercion by the powerful to maintain the illusion of a stable, well-integrated society.

9. The Marxist view of social change restricts people to a passive role in responding to inevitable cycles or changes in material culture.

10. Those with a disproportionate share of society's wealth, status, and power generally have a vested interest in preserving the status quo.

11. Conflict theorists argue that in a capitalistic economic system, many companies are not willing to pay the price to meet strict safety standards.

12. From a functionalist perspective, there is the ever-present danger that a society's most powerful groups will use technological advances to invade the privacy of the less powerful, and thereby maintain or intensify various forms of inequality and injustice.

13. One concern of the oversight committee appointed to deal with ethical, legal, and social issues raised by the Human Genome Project is to ensure that everyone who donates their genes to the project will do so voluntarily, after being informed of the risks and benefits.

14. Residents of countries in the European Union have been almost uniformly comfortable with genetically modified food.

15. Today's immigrants rely primarily on foreign-language newspapers to keep up with events at home.

MULTIPLE-CHOICE QUESTIONS: Read each question carefully and then select the best answer.

1. Which sociological perspective emphasizes that social movements provide a training ground for leaders of the political establishment?
    a. the functionalist perspective
    b. the conflict perspective
    c. the interactionist perspective
    d. labeling theory

2. You are a student and do not own a car. All of your close friends who are attending your college or university have vehicles of their own. You feel downtrodden and dissatisfied. You are experiencing
    a. relative deprivation.
    b. resource mobilization.
    c. false consciousness.
    d. depression.

3. The resource mobilization perspective would be interested in the influence of _____ on social movements.
    a. tenacity
    b. desire
    c. emotion
    d. money

4. The text observes that it takes more than desire to start a social movement: It helps to have money, access to the media, and workers. The ways in which a social movement utilizes such things are referred to collectively as
    a. relative deprivation.
    b. false consciousness.
    c. resource mobilization.
    d. economic independence.

5. Which of the following held that social movement leaders must help workers overcome feelings of false consciousness?
    a. Max Weber
    b. Émile Durkheim
    c. Robert Merton
    d. Karl Marx

6. Organized collective activities that address values and social identities, as well as improvements in the quality of life, are referred to as
    a. new social movements.
    b. social revolutions.
    c. resource mobilization.
    d. crazes.

7. Which of the following statements is NOT true?
    a. New social movements generally view the government as their ally in the struggle for a better society.
    b. Scholars of social movements now realize that gender can affect even the way we view organized efforts to resist or bring about change.
    c. Social movements grow and give birth to other movements, work in coalition with other movements, and influence each other indirectly through their effects on the larger cultural and political environment.
    d. Leadership is a central factor in the mobilization of the discontented into social movements.

8. Which of the following is an example of a new social movement?
    a. the lesbian and gay rights movement
    b. the peace movement
    c. the environmental movement
    d. all the above

9. The text cites which of the following as a recognized definition of social change?
    a. tumultuous, revolutionary alterations that lead to changes in leadership
    b. a significant alteration over time in behavior patterns and culture
    c. regular alterations in a consistent social frame of reference
    d. subtle alterations in any social system

10. Nineteenth-century theories of social change reflect the pioneering work in biological evolution done by
    a. Albert Einstein.
    b. Charles Darwin.
    c. Harriet Martineau.
    d. Benjamin Franklin.

11. The writings of Auguste Comte and Émile Durkheim are examples of
    a. cyclical theory.
    b. evolutionary theory.
    c. interactionist theory.
    d. conflict theory.

12. According to _____ theory, social change moves society in a definite direction, frequently from simple to more complex.
    a. cyclical
    b. conflict
    c. functionalist
    d. evolutionary

13. According to Talcott Parsons's _____ model, as changes occur in one part of society, there must be adjustments in other parts.
    a. disruption
    b. equilibrium
    c. conflict
    d. interactionist

14. The acceptance of preventative medicine (i.e., society has broadened its view of health care) is an example of the process that Parsons called
    a. differentiation.
    b. value generalization.
    c. inclusion.
    d. adaptive upgrading.

15. Which of the following theorists argued that conflict is a normal and desirable aspect of social change?
    a. Karl Marx
    b. Talcott Parsons
    c. Émile Durkheim
    d. all of the above

16. The term *vested interests* was coined by social economist
    a. William F. Ogburn.
    b. Talcott Parsons.
    c. Auguste Comte.
    d. Thorstein Veblen.

17. The abbreviation "NIMBY" stands for "not in my backyard," a cry often heard when people protest
    a. landfills
    b. prisons
    c. nuclear power facilities
    d. all of the above

18. Which of the following is an example of nonmaterial culture?
    a. ideas
    b. inventions
    c. social organizations
    d. communications

19. Which sociologist introduced the concept of culture lag?
    a. William F. Ogburn
    b. Talcott Parsons
    c. Auguste Comte
    d. Thorstein Veblen

20. In France during the 1800s, angry workers threw their wooden shoes into factory machinery to destroy it, thereby giving rise to the term
    a. "throw a monkey wrench into it."
    b. "wooden heart."
    c. "sabotage."
    d. "Luddites."

21.   Which of the following is NOT a common complaint of the typical neo-Luddite?
  a.   federal barriers to advancements in biotechnology
  b.   the incessant expansion of industrialization
  c.   the increasing destruction of the natural and agrarian world
  d.   the "throw away" mentality of contemporary capitalism

22.   Which perspective would say that new computer and communications technology brings with it the danger that the most powerful groups in society will use technology to violate the privacy of the less powerful?
  a.   the functionalist perspective
  b.   the conflict perspective
  c.   the interactionist perspective
  d.   none of the above

23.   The term *Frankenfood* refers to_____.
  a.   fodder for genetically modified cows and pigs
  b.   toxic corn
  c.   genetically modified food, from breakfast cereal to fresh vegetables
  d.   food or low nutritional value

24.   Which term refers to an immigrant who sustains multiple social relationships that link his or her society of origin with the society of settlement?
  a.   transnational
  b.   transglobal
  c.   global citizen
  d.   none of the above

25.   Which sociological perspective sees transnationals as a way for economies to maximize their use of human labor?
  a.   the functionalist perspective
  b.   the conflict perspective
  c.   the interactionist perspective
  d.   the feminist perspective

FILL-IN QUESTIONS: Fill in the blank spaces in the sentences below with the correct words. Where two or more words are required, there will be a corresponding number of blank spaces.

1.   Herbert Blumer defined _____ _____ as "collective enterprises to establish a new order of life."

2.   The _____ perspective emphasizes that even when unsuccessful, social movements contribute to the formation of public opinion.

3.   The term relative deprivation recognizes the importance of _____ in the emergence of social movements.

4.   A relatively deprived person is dissatisfied because he or she feels deprived relative to some appropriate _____ group.

5.   As Max Weber described it in 1904, _____ is the quality of an individual that sets him or her apart from ordinary people.

6.   As Robert Michels pointed out, social movements often become more _____ over time.

7.   The SSKKMS movement in India was unusual when compared to other social movements in the region in that about half of its participants, and many of its leaders, were _____.

8.   Early evolutionary theorists concluded in a(n) _____ fashion that their own behavior and culture were more advanced than those of earlier civilizations.

9.   Talcott Parsons used the term _____ to refer to the increasing complexity of social organization.

10.   As the work of Talcott Parsons demonstrates, the _____ perspective has made a distinctive contribution to the study of social change.

11.   _____ _____ argued that conflict is a normal and desirable aspect of social change.

12.   Social economist _____ _____ coined the term "vested interests" to refer to those people or groups who will suffer in the event of social change, and who have a stake in maintaining the status quo.

13.   William Ogburn introduced the concept of culture lag to refer to the period of maladjustment during which the _____ culture is still struggling to adapt to new _____ conditions.

14.   The term _____ refers to those who are wary of technological innovations, and who question the incessant expansion of industrialization, the increasing destruction of the natural and agrarian world, and the "throw it away" mentality of contemporary capitalism.

15.   The internet's _____, a new form of social networking, allow organizers of social movements to enlist like-minded people with relatively little effort and expense.

UNDERSTANDING SOCIAL POLICY: Each of the following questions is based on material that appears in the social policy section on "Transnationals." Write a brief answer to each question in the space provided below.

1.   How has globalization impacted the world labor market?

2.   What is the conflict view of transnationals?

3.   What voting rights do transnationals typically have?

DEFINITIONS OF KEY TERMS

Social change: Significant alteration over time in behavior patterns and culture, including norms and values.

Social movement: An organized collective activity to bring about or resist fundamental change in an existing group or society.

Relative deprivation: The conscious feeling of a negative discrepancy between legitimate expectations and present actualities.

Resource mobilization: The ways in which a social movement utilizes such resources as money, political influence, access to the media, and personnel.

False consciousness: A term used by Karl Marx to describe an attitude held by members of a class that does not accurately reflect their objective position.

New social movement: An organized collective activity that addresses values and social identities, as well as improvements in the quality of life.

Evolutionary theory: A theory of social change that holds that society is moving in a definite direction.

Equilibrium model: The functionalist view that society tends toward a state of stability or balance.

Vested interests: Those people or groups who will suffer in the event of social change, and who have a stake in maintaining the status quo.

Culture lag: A period of maladjustment when the nonmaterial culture is still struggling to adapt to new material conditions.

Luddites: Rebellious craft workers in 19th-century England who destroyed new factory machinery as part of their resistance to the industrial revolution.

Transnational: An immigrant who sustains multiple social relationships that link his or her society of origin with the society of settlement.

ANSWERS TO SELF-TEST

Modified True/False Questions

1. True
2. True
3. In our male-dominated society, women find it more difficult than men to assume leadership positions in social movement organizations.
4. Whereas traditional views of social movements tended to emphasize resource mobilization on a local level, new social movements theory offers a broad, global perspective on social and political activism.
5. The leadership core of the SSKKMS social movement contained a number of women.
6. True

7. Talcott Parsons's approach to social change explicitly incorporates the evolutionary notion of continuing progress.

8. As noted by critics, the functionalist approach virtually disregards the use of coercion by the powerful to maintain the illusion of a stable, well-integrated society.

9. The Marxist view of social change does not restrict people to a passive role in responding to inevitable cycles or changes in material culture.

10. True

11. True

12. From a conflict perspective, there is the ever-present danger that a society's most powerful groups will use technological advances to invade the privacy of the less powerful.

13. True

14. Controversy concerning genetically modified food began in Europe and spread to other countries, including the U. S.

15. In generations past, immigrants read foreign-language newspapers to keep in touch with events in their home countries. Today, the Internet gives immigrants immediate access to their countries and kinfolk.

Multiple-Choice Questions

1. a	10. b	19. a
2. a	11. b	20. c
3. d	12. d	21. a
4. c	13. b	22. b
5. d	14. b	23. c
6. a	15. a	24. a
7. a	16. d	25. a
8. d	17. d	
9. b	18. a	

Fill-In Questions

1. social movements	9. differentiation
2. functionalist	10. functionalist
3. perception	11. Marx
4. reference	12. Thorstein Veblen
5. charisma	13. nonmaterial; material
6. bureaucratic	14. neo-Luddites
7. women	15. chatrooms
8. ethnocentric	

Understanding Social Policy: Transnationals

1. Despite legal restrictions, the labor market has become an increasingly global one. Just as globalization has integrated government policies, cultures, social movements, and financial markets, it has unified what once were discrete national labor markets.

2. Conflict theorists charge that globalization and international migration have increased the economic gulf between developed and developing nations. In addition, through tourism and the global reach of the mass media, people in poorer countries have become aware of the affluent lifestyle common in developed nations—and, of course, many of them now aspire to it. Sociologists who follow the world systems analysis suggest that the global flow of people, not just goods and resources, should be factored into the theoretical relationship between core and periphery nations.

3. Voter eligibility is an unresolved transnational issue. Not all nations allow dual citizenship, and even those countries that do allow it may not allow absent nationals to vote. The United States and Great Britain are rather liberal in this regard, permitting dual citizenship and allowing émigrés to continue to vote. Mexico, in contrast, has been reluctant to allow citizens who have emigrated to vote.